MOUNTAIN 10.

Climbing the Labyrinth Within

GARY BOELHOWER
JOE MIGUEZ
TRICIA PEARCE

5.5
Mountain 10: Climbing the Labyrinth Within

Printed in the United States of America.

CreateSpace, An Amazon.com Company
North Charleston, South Carolina

ISBN-10: 1481126997
EAN-13: 978-1481126991

Library of Congress Control Number: 2012922911
CreateSpace Independent Publishing Platform
North Charleston, SC

Publisher: Mountain 10 Resources
www.mountainten.com

Mountain 10. and LABgraphic are trademarks of Mountain Ten Resources. Application has been made for national and international registry.

Mountain 10 LABgraphic designs by Joe Miguez.
Digital enhancement of LABgraphic designs by Matt Kania (www.maphero.com)

Photo credits:
Front cover and photos on pages 41, 63 by istock photo.
Photos on pages 2, 16, 28, 31, 81 by Jeff Saward.
Photo of Gary Boelhower by Amanda Hansmeyer (www.shutterstoriesonline.com)
Photo of Joe Miguez by Sarah Sturges
Photo of Tricia Pearce by Roger H. Brown

CONTENTS

Gratitude vii

Prologue 1

Chapter One: Wisdom Within 5

Chapter Two: Wisdom Technologies Ancient and New 21

Chapter Three: Preparing for Mountain 10. 37

Chapter Four: Mountain 10. 47

Chapter Five: Mountain 10. Change Cycle 61

Chapter Six: Continuing the Journey 77

Notes, Bibliography, Recommended Reading........................... 89

About the Authors 95

DEDICATION

We dedicate this book
To all the seekers who came before us
clothed in courage and gifting us with wisdom.

To those who stand with us now
and walk on either side of us with support and challenge.

To those who will come after our journeys are ended
and will keep the flame of curiosity and passion burning.

GRATITUDE

I am deeply grateful to Parker Palmer for writing eloquently about listening to the inner teacher and demonstrating effective ways to access interior wisdom; to Virginia Gilmore for responding to the call of Sophia and inviting me on the journey; to Pamela Mittlefehldt for unflagging support in the writing process and insightful editing; to my leadership group Gary Baltz, Timothy Haukeness and Barry Mulholland for constancy, accountability and "clipping in." To my husband, Gary Anderson, for the daily connections that keep me asking questions and leaning toward the light.

Gary Boelhower

In gratitude for supporting my "thread" ("The Way It Is" by William Stafford): Rolf Smith, Mike Donahue, Judi Neal, Marian Their, Anthony Hyatt, Matteo Catullo, Paolo Sbuttoni, Bill Olsen, David Horth, Bill Costa, Steve Dahlberg, John Fredricks, Bill Shepard, Robert Ferre, Chris Brewer, Mary Murdock, Gregg Fraley, Caroline Palek, Cy Rinkle, Creative Problem Solving Institute, Message Company.

Joe Miguez

My sincere gratitude and love to my mother, Edith Pearce, and my grandmother, Mary Lee Girrbach for nurturing me from child to woman with constant love, strength, and wisdom; to my family for gifts of unconditional love, especially Dylan, Kylee, Noah and Haley for their eagerness to learn and invitations to play; to friends woven throughout my life offering abundant encouragement; to those who have walked paths alongside mine sharing diverse gifts; and to special others standing near who tenderly hold my fragile pieces when I need to slow down. Thank God, for giving me the courage to ask questions and to seek the answer – YES.

Tricia Pearce

In deep gratitude for each other and in celebration of "we three."

Gary, Joe, Tricia

PROLOGUE

We three, Gary Boelhower, Joe Miguez and Tricia Pearce, invite you into a process for exploring your inner wisdom that we have found life-changing and life-giving. We have been facilitating the investigation of personal and organizational wisdom for many years. We believe every person and every organization has the most important answers about purpose and values within them. All people have a deep source of profound and simple wisdom. This book provides a technology or instrument called Mountain 10 that is designed to help you access your wisdom.

Technology refers to the application of knowledge or science to any human activity. We most often think of technology in terms of machines and computers. However, whenever we utilize or implement information or knowledge we are involved in technology. The knowledge takes concrete form, has concrete impact or application. It is no longer simply an idea but has been translated into a model, machine or process. Mountain 10 is a technology to delve into our inner wisdom. We call this technology Mountain 10 because mountain climbing is an apt metaphor for the effort and excitement involved in the process of touching one's own inner wisdom. Of course, we won't be climbing a mountain. We will be tracing a path on paper, a LABgraphic, based on the labyrinth laid in the floor of the 13th century Chartres Cathedral in Chartres, France. It is called a LABgraphic because it is a labyrinth path and a laboratory space intentionally created for our self-observation, experimentation, testing our own wisdom, and entering the inner geography of our own story. The Mountain 10 process will take us along a pathway that has been well worn but is new to each person's particular way of stepping and searching.

This is not an easy climb. The way up a mountain is never straight. The LABgraphic path is recursive and involves the iterative process of switching back and forth. It takes time, attention and intention. However, we know the technology works. It is based on the ancient labyrinths, mandalas and pathways that can be found across cultures and ages around the globe. In every epoch, people have used similar technologies to listen deeply to the heart's longing, to our highest calling.

Labyrinth petroglyph in Arroyo Hondo, New Mexico This photo is one of many occurrences of the labyrinth symbol in the Southwestern United States and the northern states of Mexico. It is not clear when the symbol first reached this region but it is an important theme in the traditional stories of the Hopi, Akimel, O'odham, Tohono O'odham and Yaqui peoples.

Mountain 10 will help us get in touch with our own creative source and core values. It is a tool for paying attention to your inner journey. Just as the external world provides endless sights to explore, the inner world is rich with diverse terrains and treasures. Mountain 10 will give us a map for the interior journey, a space for self-exploration. Joe and Tricia developed this dangerously-safe space as they worked with diverse individuals, groups and organizations to reap the fruits of the labyrinth reflective process.

Tricia is a principal and cofounder of the LAByrinth Xperience™. The defining moment for the idea of Mountain 10 comes from Tricia's experience within the labyrinth. She has fine-tuned the Mountain 10 technology with large and small groups, in contexts as diverse as education, healthcare, publishing, manufacturing and spiritual renewal. She has used labyrinths in programs for businesses, conferences and retreat centers across the United States and around the world. She currently works as a consultant, facilitator and coach. Her clients include the American Hospital Association, American Cancer Society, Association of Volunteer Administration, CREA World Conference on Creativity and Innovation, Creative Problem Solving Institute, International Congress of Accelerated Learning, and International Alliance for Learning.

Joe is a principal and co-founder of the LAByrinth Xperience. Mountain 10 is grounded in Joe's pioneering work in applying the technology of the labyrinth to innovation and creativity in business and other organizations. He has been instrumental in reframing the ancient concept of the labyrinth into an emergent model for accessing the wisdom of organizations and individuals. He is a founding member of the Labyrinth Society and served on its first board of directors. He has presented workshops throughout the world informed by his experience as an art educator and TV director. His clients include Dupont, Area Energy, DeAgostini Publishing Group, IT, Exxon, Federal Express, EURO RSGQ worldwide, University of Tennessee leadership program, New Haven University MBA leadership program, Union Institute and University, and the Center for Creative Leadership, among others.

Gary has taught ethics, spirituality, and leadership at the high school, undergraduate and graduate levels for forty years. He has also filled leadership roles in higher education as chair of humanities, dean of life-long learning, dean of graduate studies, vice president for academic affairs and co-founder and first director of the Center for Spirituality and Leadership at Marian University. He has consulted with a broad range of organizations and has facilitated executive development programs on dialogue, authentic leadership, values and vision, professional ethics and the respectful workplace. The constant throughout these various roles has been his interest in the internal yearning for what is good and true. After experiencing the labyrinth several times, he met Joe at the Center for Creative Leadership where they were both giving keynote presentations on aspects of leadership with spirit. Their collaboration and continuing conversation led to this book.

We three have reflected together on every word, sentence and paragraph of this book to achieve a thoughtful consensus. It has not been easy. We have learned a great deal about patience, respect and listening to our own inner wisdom. We have observed our own shortcomings and genius. We have let go of our own assumptions and mental models again and again. We have persisted in our vision of bringing Mountain 10 to a wider audience. The fact that you are reading this prologue is proof that dreamers can work together to realize their vision.

In writing this book, we experienced four dimensions of the change process--awareness, letting go, vision and realization--aspects of the natural, human process of ongoing transformation. These elements of change will be introduced in chapter three as you prepare for your Mountain 10 exploration.

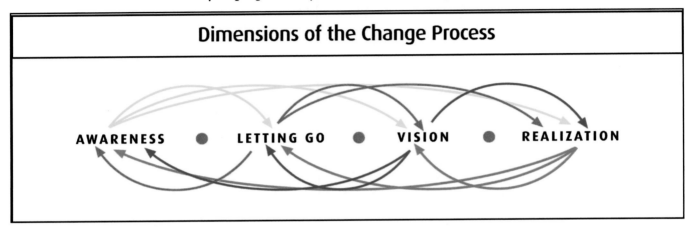

Dimensions of the Change Process

AWARENESS   LETTING GO   VISION   REALIZATION

In chapter four, you will experience the Mountain 10 climb using the LAB-graphic based on the eleven-circuit labyrinth. Chapter five offers an adaptation of Mountain 10 that is meant for seasoned climbers. After you have experienced Mountain 10 a few times, you may want to add further dimensions to your internal exploration, and experience Mountain 10 Change Cycle. The final chapter provides some reflections on the integration process, on realizing the wisdom and vision you accessed on your climb. We begin the book with two chapters that provide important background information on the ancient technologies that cultures have used throughout the ages to touch the wisdom of the heart. This is the theory that undergirds the technology; it explains why the tool works. Of course, you don't have to know the physics of the Bernoulis principle to captain a sailboat but many people are interested in knowing the *why* behind what works.

There are a few times throughout these chapters when the individual experience or creative expression of one of us is communicated. In these instances, we simply use our first names to identify the experience or the piece of poetry. We have worked hard to create a book that is inviting and accessible. In this effort we often use "we" and "our" as well as "you" and "your" in the same section. Although this is somewhat unconventional, we hope it helps you to see yourself on this journey with us. We hope your Mountain 10 climb and return leads to insight and ultimately to what you really want out of life. Although we are honored to be your guides on this journey, we are also fellow travelers and we would love to hear from you at www. MountainTen.com.

Chapter 1:
WISDOM WITHIN

The human search for wisdom is never ending. In every age and epoch, we find the remnants of this eternal quest in proverbs, stories and sayings. We also find evidence of the processes that individuals, organizations and communities used to connect to the source of wisdom—the council fire, the philosophical dialogue, the pilgrimage, the labyrinth, and in our own time, the various methods for systems thinking, whole brain learning, effective and affective problem solving, and imaginative innovation. In these pages we introduce a new technology for practical wisdom—Mountain 10. It is grounded in ancient traditions and draws from contemporary achievements. It combines the metaphor of climbing to the summit with the myth of the odyssey journey. Mountain 10 is a laboratory space of experimentation, patterned after the iterative process of the labyrinth, a dangerously safe space of possibility for observing and exploring one's inner wisdom. You are the critical variable in this laboratory experiment, the uniqueness of your story, questions and vision. Mountain 10 provides a blueprint for navigating your future. It doesn't provide an answer from outside but a way for you to access your own best answer from the inside of your own wisdom.

> It is not the mountain we conquer, but ourselves.
>
> **Edmund Hillary**

The quest for wisdom is particularly important in our present age of data gluttony and information overstimulation. It is easy to get trapped in the fallacy of more equals better: more data equals better decisions, more stuff equals a better life. If we just read one more self-help book or listen to one more self-esteem program, we will find the answer to a happier life. If we just bring one more expert consultant into the organization, our problems will be solved. Leaders in our organizations are often taught and expected to deal with the "hard" stuff, making data-driven decisions based on labor costs, profit margins, and market share. The "soft" stuff is disdained as a distraction from the real tasks at hand. Yet, anyone who has filled a leadership position knows that the "soft" stuff is really the most difficult part of leadership— whether in an organization, a non-profit board, a committee, or a family. There is no algorithm to figure out the gains from investing in another human being. There is no formula for mixing encouragement and vision and openness to achieve a sense of common purpose and a motivating mission.

> To work in the world lovingly means that we are defining what we will be for, rather than reacting to what we are against.
>
> **Christina Baldwin**

It may be helpful to understand personality types and conflict resolution strategies, but no toolbox of techniques will provide the sensitive, intuitive grasp of another person's resistance or frustration. Ultimately we are faced again and again with the difficult task of figuring out the appropriate response in a specific situation. How does one gain this empathic identification with another that deepens understanding? How does one know how to weigh the various elements of a difficult dilemma? How does one make the choice that responds to our deepest values and opens us to new possibilities? No self-help toolbox or set of management skills will provide the kind of self-awareness that leads to insight and creative response. The authentic response to the challenges of life comes from accessing the profound inner wisdom that dwells within each one of us. To live and lead congruently is a constant, difficult challenge. It requires that each one of us not lose touch with our most deeply held ideals or heartfelt passions.

The key shift that must occur in our individual and organizational lives is to trust our own wisdom. Rather than focusing our attention outward, we are called to listen to the inner teacher, to the wisdom within. We are called to be attentive to our own internal journey and to reap the harvest of our own experience. Our thoughts and feelings, our bodily knowing, our creative leaps and artistic urges contain all the clues we need to discover a more purposeful life and build a more spirit-filled and productive workplace.

Integrating Body, Mind and Spirit

You were born with greatness.

You were born with wings.

You were not meant for crawling, so don't.

You have wings,

Learn to use them and fly.

Rumi

Yes, we need information and statistics and experts. However, accessing the hard data is the easy part, at least in comparison to the more difficult work of clarifying values and principles. Living authentically requires paying attention to body, mind and spirit wholeness. It requires integrating information and values, data and dreams, "what is" and "what if." This is the hard part—application, implementation, living it out. This is wisdom and it requires the assimilation of knowledge, values and action.

Anyone who has ever attempted to teach someone else—whether a parent teaching a child, an instructor teaching a student, or a trainer teaching a new employee—knows that the "proof is in the pudding." The simple ability to reiterate or repeat an idea or a set of instructions is not enough to prove learning. Only when children make their own wise decisions does the parent know that key values have been communicated. Only when the student is able to apply a theory or practice a skill does the teacher know that learning has occurred. Only when the new employee is able to do the job can the trainer be sure the training has been successful. We also know that learners are always teachers who bring their own perspectives, insights, and experiences into the learning exchange. Every good teacher is a fellow learner who sees new insights through the teaching-learning process.

The ultimate end of learning is not only information but formation, not only new knowledge but a new way of being and doing. The ancient Greeks termed this new way of being and doing *phronesis, practical wisdom*. Wisdom requires that our knowing informs our identity and our actions in the world. For instance, the cognitive concept of justice must be translated into fairness within a family, the larger community and the global society. Without the translation into action there is no wisdom. Wisdom doesn't happen in the mind alone or through the mind alone. Rather, wisdom is a way of being and doing that integrates mind, body and spirit.

Our Western culture has focused almost exclusively on mental knowing and the mind as the instrument of knowledge. Only recently have we begun to value the Eastern traditions which holistically integrate knowledge that comes from body, mind and spirit. The Western medical model still treats diseases and parts of the body. Even when there is an intentional focus on the whole person, there is often a division of labor with the physician treating the body, the social worker treating the feelings and family system, and the chaplain treating the spirit. In contrast, the article "A Body-Mind-Spirit Model in Health: An Eastern Approach" explains that health in Eastern traditions, "…is perceived as a harmonious equilibrium that exists between the interplay of 'yin' and 'yang': the five internal elements (metal, wood, water, fire and earth), the six environmental conditions (dry, wet, hot, cold, wind and flame), other external sources of harm (physical injury, insect bites, poison, overeat and overwork), and the seven emotions (joy, sorrow, anger, worry, panic, anxiety and fear)."[1]

Slowly we are learning the importance of body-mind-spirit integration. We are coming to understand the essential need for holistic, applied, everyday, practical wisdom. This realization is coming primarily through our wounds. There are deep scars in our personal psyches from attempting to deny the beauty and natural inclinations and clear messages of our bodies. There are gaping wounds in our organizations where a mechanistic view of persons and work suppresses the spirit and vitality of persons. Severe tensions strain our social fabric because of the increasing accumulation of wealth by a few while nearly one-half of the world's population does not have enough nutritious food or pure water. Looking at the world as if it were a village of just 100 people helps us understand how our social fabric is torn, stretched and straining.[2]

I certainly believe that being in contact with one's spirit and nurturing one's spirit is as important as nurturing one's body and mind. We are three dimensional beings: body, mind, spirit.

Laurence Fishburne

IF THE WORLD WERE 100 PEOPLE

50 would be female, 50 would be male

26 would be children, 74 would be adults,
8 of whom would be 65 and older

There would be:
60 Asians, 11 Europeans, 15 Africans, 14 people from the Americas

There would be:
33 Christians, 22 Muslims, 14 Hindus, 7 Buddhists, 12 people who practice other religions, 12 people who would not be aligned with a religion

12 would speak Chinese, 5 would speak Spanish, 5 would speak English
3 would speak Hindi, 3 would speak Arabic, 3 would speak Bengali 3 would speak
Portuguese, 2 would speak Russian, 2 would speak Japanese, 62 would speak other
languages

83 would be able to read and write, 17 would not

7 would have a college degree, 22 would own or share a computer

77 people would have a place to shelter them from the wind and the rain,
but 23 would not

1 would be dying of starvation
15 would be undernourished
21 would be overweight
87 would have access to safe drinking water
13 people would have no clean, safe water to drink

The earth itself is groaning under the weight of our lack of wise stewardship. We need wisdom. We need it now.

So, where should we seek it? What expert should we call on our cell phones? What are the key words to enter into our search engines that will bring the answer? Our tendency is to search for an answer outside ourselves, to think that someone else must have figured it out already. We believe that our own hearts aren't full enough to teach us the answers. Wisdom calls us to journey inward, to find a sanctuary of silence where we might have a conversation with our better selves, a conversation that will pay attention to what our feelings are saying, what our body is telling us, what our heart is aching for.

SANCTUARY (by Gary Boelhower)[3]

*Right here in this small
bright clearing among
the reaching emerald branches,
I plant my heart like the seed
of everything possible, everything
to hope for, to believe in.*

*Right here where the sweet
sweat of earth rises from this mulch
of moss and decaying needles,
from this mix of shit and stardust,
and mingles with the stinging scent*

of pine. The tall trunks sway
like the hot hips of God in their
birthing dance and the vital
vernix of spring seeps from
every pore in the warming bark.

This is the Eden of desire, the genesis
garden where a heart can break
open like a promise, where a body
can stretch its endless longings
and trust the river of its own blood.

This is the original story, before
the tree of knowledge, before we made
the jealous gods in the image of our
fears, before the curse of shame.
This is the garden of grace, the long
sigh of belonging, breath of home.

Wisdom calls us home to the fullness of who we are. It asks us what we really want. It tells us to trust our own experience, to pay attention to how its voice echoes in the fierce flutes of our own bones. Wisdom reminds us to seek the sanctuary of our own silence and have faith that we can figure it out.

It is not easy to listen to the voice within rather than to the brain on top. Benjamin Hoff in *The Tao of Pooh* puts it this way:

> Is it really Brain that takes us where we need to go? Or is it all too often Brain that sends us off in the wrong direction, following the echo of the wind in the treetops, which we think is real, rather than listening to the voice within us that tells us which way to turn?[4]

We are not advocating the separation of intellect from intuition but, rather, are calling for a deeper attention to interior reflection, balancing the mind and the heart, scientific reasoning and artistic sensitivity, information from outside and guidance from inside.

Many persons in our contemporary Western culture have an aversion to reflection, and leaders especially find it difficult to embrace a more reflective approach. In *Let Your Life Speak*, Parker Palmer reminds us that leaders in our contemporary society "tend toward extroversion, which often means ignoring what is happening inside ourselves. … Leaders need not only the technical skills to manage the external world but also the spiritual skills to journey inward toward the source of both shadow and light."[5]

Listening is such a simple act. We just have to be willing to sit there and listen. If we can do that we create moments in which real healing is available.

Margaret Wheatley

Developing more attentive reflective listening to our own wisdom involves working against the grain of our culture, swimming upstream against the current of our personal comfort. Accessing inner wisdom will require that we check our old habits of automatically turning on the radio, CD player, television, computer, and checking our text messages rather than listening in silence to the voice within. It will require that we stop to ask questions and listen deeply to those with whom we live and work, rather than exchange surface pleasantries and conditioned, acceptable responses. This transformed, inside-out way of living balances external attentiveness and internal sensitivity. It demands that we schedule time to be alone, to retreat into nature, to check in with our own feelings and to consider how our actions fit with our values and vision. Giving priority time to reflection is not an easy adjustment. Even those convinced of the need for silence to listen to the inner teacher find it difficult to do.

Our educational systems and training agendas are clearly focused on externals. Reflection is neither prized nor taught. Very often, we see an overemphasis on answers, rather than on the multi-faceted exploration of key questions. Wisdom requires an attitude that loves questions and values the balance between reflection and action. Rainer Maria Rilke, in his *Letters to a Young Poet*, expresses an attitude toward questions that invites wisdom. He says, "Try to love the questions themselves, like locked rooms and like books written in a foreign language. "[6] This attitude of loving questions seems contrary to the sense of urgency that is often experienced when persons and organizations are faced with critical issues that need wise decisions. Rilke's words point to a respect for questions themselves. It is not only patience that he espouses here but also an attitude of acceptance and valuation regarding the questions.

Learning to Love the Questions

Wise persons enlarge the space in their lives for questions, for expanding awareness. This positive attitude toward questions seems to come naturally to children. Tricia tells of reading *Elfie* with her granddaughter, Kylee, age seven. They hooked their pinkie fingers together and promised to read the whole book out loud to each other. The book poses the question, "What is wisdom?" in contrast to "What does it mean to be smart?". Elfie, the main character, begins thinking, "to be wise is to be deep, like an ocean is deep. A person can be smart and that's all. But another person can be deep, and then they're called wise."[7] Later in the book, Elfie continues to muse about wisdom:

> I used to say to myself, 'If only I could think clearly!' That was because I didn't know any answers. But now I think that giving the right answers is not so important. What's important is being able to ask the right questions. Or is it being able to ask questions right? Or

could it be both? … 'That's *it!*' I say to myself, 'if you're *smart,* you think about how *much* you know; if you're *wise,* you think about how *little* you know.'[8]

Tricia's granddaughter piped up at the end of the book, "And now we know about wisdom." It is imperative to be able to create an open space where we can truly consider, converse and reflect. We must have the courage to admit how little we know and how much we need to learn. This is especially true for adults living and working within a context of urgency.

To live in the open space of the question, we need to make friends with silence and solitude. Our present culture tends to fill up any empty moment with auditory and visual stimulation. We seem to be running away from our uniqueness, denying the essence of who we are as human beings. What differentiates us from all the other animals is our unique ability for self-reflection. We have the capacity to ask probing questions of ourselves, to search for new meanings and to dream new visions for ourselves and our world. The question is do we have the courage to engage in this search and realize these visions.

When we stop listening to our inner voice, we stop being human. We stop taking our unique place in the universe. We shrug off our particular responsibility in the world. When we stop creating space and time to hear the longings of our hearts and the creative imaginings of our spirits, we stop doing what we alone can do. This point was driven home to Gary in an experience with his daughter. He delights in telling the following story:

> One day, after looking everywhere, I found my daughter, Rebecca, sitting in the dark on the stairway to the basement. When I opened the door, there she was crouching in the silent darkness with her head in her hands. I thought something must be wrong. Had she gotten into a fight with one of her friends? Did I say something that hurt her feelings? Was she facing some difficult challenge? When I asked what was the matter, her response startled me. She said, "Dad, I'm just thinking about my mind thinking." She was four years old.

Anyone who has raised a child knows that questioning is part of the essence of who we are as human beings, that reflection is part of our hard wiring. Around the age of three, children start asking why. At first, the question is asked incessantly. Most parents in our culture are not comfortable with the question. After the third or fourth "why," the response is usually, "Because I said so." or "That's just the way it is." But children don't give up. There seems to be an internal drive to keep going deeper, to take the question to the next level, to understand things at their roots. An attentive parent can almost hear the processing going on. They witness the quizzical looks and the surprising realizations on their children's faces.

Keep away from the wisdom which does not cry, the philosophy which does not laugh, and the greatness which does not bow before children.

Khalil Gibran

Values at Our Core

Are we denying our true selves by not encouraging reflection and taking time for silence? Margaret Wheatley, pioneer in applying new paradigms of science to leadership and organizations, believes that leaders must value reflection and take the time to think. She says,

> We cannot create the future we want by increasing the speed of change, by increasing the hurriedness and the franticness… At some point, it's up to us to say, 'We must take time to think; we must take time to reflect'.…It's a revolutionary act to reflect these days. It's not in our job description. Luckily, it's in our species description. What frustrates me so much is understanding the great gift of human consciousness and the ability to notice and to reflect and to learn, and then to see how we are pretending that is not our gift to the planet.[9]

Exploring the depths of our own questions and accessing our own inner wisdom is not new; we've simply forgotten in our age of scientism and consumption the ancient and perennial traditions of wisdom.

With deep reflection and silence, in the sanctuary where we listen to our personal call, we get in touch with the values that are at the core of who we are as individuals and as participating members of our organizations. Values can be defined as our key priorities or motivating principles. When we focus on values, we turn our attention to the deeper questions of "why" and "who." The why question gets at the values that are the basis or foundation for making decisions. These values and beliefs, in large part, define who I am.

Ultimately, one chooses actions based on self identity, on the "who" one is as person and leader.

Leadership, management and education experts are only beginning to understand the importance of identity, character and integrity. For many years, the Western tradition has emphasized the "what" and "how," or the functions of work and the skills of professions. For instance, good leadership has been defined largely in terms of behaviors: developing vision, creating plans, projecting market response, communicating effectively, engineering and re-engineering the processes for production or service. The focus of leadership has been on developing strategies, methods and models for how to engage in each of these important organizational behaviors to bring about the desired outcome. Although these functions of leadership are critical to organizational success, they are of secondary importance. When we face ourselves in life's mirror, the persistent, recurrent questions that a leader or teacher or healthcare professional must ask are "Who am I?" "Where am I?" "What do I want?" and "Why do I choose to act as I do?"

Warren Bennis in his leadership classic *On Becoming a Leader* emphasizes the need for self-knowledge. He writes, "But until you truly know yourself, strengths and weaknesses, know what you want to do and why you want to do it, you cannot succeed in any but the most superficial sense of the word."[10]

The doors we open and close each day decide the lives we live.

Flora Whittemore

When we are living in a way that connects with our values, we are able to live a richer, more integrated life. When there is a match between soul and work, between what we really believe and the activity that fills the largest part of our days, there is a deep satisfaction about our lives. We've all seen people whose work matched their identity, values and gifts. We come away from those encounters with a sense that these persons were meant for this particular occupation. There's a fit between their heart and what they are doing, between their core values and their work. Gary tells of his interactions with students in his course, "Renewing the Inner Teacher," that exhibit this idea of coherence between values and work.

> I have the opportunity to hear teachers talk about the connections between their soul and their work. For some, it is crystal clear they are doing what they were called to do in life. They daily live out their deepest values. They couldn't imagine not being a teacher. They tell their success stories with tears streaming down their faces.

> Linda tells me about her student Tara who started second grade with very low reading and comprehension skills, an extremely negative attitude, and almost no friends. She talks about her morning meetings before school with Tara, reading together at her desk every Tuesday and Thursday morning; about the small library of books that Linda passed on to Tara because "I had a lot of doubles on my own shelves and the used book store just about gives these things away." She talks about the changes in Tara: the amazing jump in her reading ability, her animated participation in class discussion, her new friends. And the hair ribbon that she wears every Tuesday, a gift from Linda after Tara made her first oral book report. After hearing Linda's story, I know she was born to be a teacher.

> For others, the story is different. Some talk of fatigue or burnout. They're not sure they can face another year or another difficult class. For some of them, it becomes clear that teaching doesn't fit their spirit.

The Fit Between Our Inner and Outer Selves

This concept of "fit" is one that arises often in organizations. We look for new employees who will "fit" with the organization's culture. We hire consultants based on the "fit" between our needs and their skills. But there is a deeper kind of "fit" that reflective leaders explore. It is the fit between the inner geography and the outer geography. Is the outer life congruent with one's most deeply held values and vision? Lack of congruence is experienced in many different ways—a nagging intuitive hunch that one's life just isn't working, sleepless nights struggling with work issues that won't go away, upset stomachs over decisions made or not made, a deep desire to want to stop everything so there is simply space and time to think. All of these feelings are indicators that there is something that is not in alignment. Something is incongruent.

When there is congruence among parts of a system or people in a team, there is natural flow. Difficult work sometimes feels effortless as the synergy flows among persons. A physical image of total congruence, balance and ease might be represented by the basketball great Michael Jordan. His intricate dynamic alignment was awesome. It would take a year to chart the biophysics of one hang gliding lay up, twisted and torqued into five different vectors before the ball is stuffed through the hoop. An extension of leg balances an extension of arm; a twist of neck and torso in opposite rotation fakes even the best guarding prophet trying to foretell the future before the flash of the camera witnesses the winning shot. That's congruence, every muscle and synapse working in intricate harmony. Congruence is an art, acquired through discipline, practice, experimentation and more discipline. It is also a deep intuitive knowing at the cellular level.

The issue of fit or congruence works at three levels. The first level is the fit between what we know about ourselves and our dreams and what we articulate to ourselves. In other words, are we clear about our deepest values? Although this level may seem simplistic, how many of us are aware of and honest about what our hearts and souls are saying to us? It's easy to get caught up in cultural expectations and consumer distractions. Sometimes we reach middle age before we seriously ask, "Is this really what I want? Is this really what makes my heart sing?" Congruence, then, requires that we be as clear as possible about the priorities at the core of our spirits. It is an interesting and provocative exercise to write your central values in a few phrases or sentences and revisit these personal words of self understanding every six months.

> The need to leave a legacy is our spiritual need to have a sense of meaning, purpose, personal congruence, and contribution.
>
> **Stephen Covey**

LEVELS OF CONGRUENCE OR "FIT"

Congruence between inner yearnings and clear articulation	Inner dreams and hopes become articulated into mission, values and plans
Congruence between personal values and behaviors	Values and priorities are lived and enacted, not perfectly but with authenticity and reflection
Congruence between personal values and organizations	Personal values and ethics are consistent with organizations where one works, worships, volunteers

The second level of congruence involves the match between values and thoughts, words and actions. Do our behaviors fit with our priorities? We all know persons who are able to articulate a set of values very well, but when it comes to living those values, they fall far short of the mark. This kind of dissonance in a leader's life is both personally and organizationally destructive. Leaders who recognize the inconsistency between their words and actions often experience significant interior conflict and personal stress. There may be a nagging feeling of dissatisfaction in their lives, a sense of being stuck, even paralyzed.

The recognition of dissonance between values and actions may result in a process of personal transformation into greater integrity or a process of disillusionment. Living in a state of significant dissonance or incongruity is difficult and consumes an inordinate amount of energy. Some persons spend their energy on rationalization or making internal excuses. For others, such dissonance floods their lives with depression and anxiety. For those who lead with integrity and attention to values, the dissonance is not significant. There is energy and joy in leading values-based work even in the face of difficulties. The minor incongruities are greeted as personal challenges. As the level of congruence between values and actions increases, a leader experiences more satisfaction and a deeper sense of meaning.

The third level of congruence is the fit between one's values and the policies, structures and culture of the organizations in which one works, volunteers, worships, etc. One might ask, "Can I be myself in this organization? Do I have to change my usual way of dealing with people to be part of this organization?" When there is consistent integration of our values in the organizations to which we are connected, we experience our places of employment, community involvement, and worship as supportive and nurturing environments. They become avenues for becoming the persons we want to be, for living out our birthright gifts in the world, for putting our passions into practice. Our work and other involvements, with all of their difficulties and challenges, become a joy. We feel like we are doing what we ought to be doing. It isn't always possible to have a significant impact on the values, policies and structures of the organizations we work, volunteer and worship in. Sometimes we don't have the freedom to walk away from organizations that are not consistent with our own values and priorities. In such situations, it is important to acknowledge the lack of congruence and to find avenues to practice our values even in small ways within our organizational contexts.

Living as Whole Beings

When there is congruence between our values and goals, between our principles and decisions, we experience a strong sense of "fit." This congruence provides the opportunity for holistic wellness, health and fitness, truly impacting body, mind and spirit. When there is a "fit" between our values and the various dimensions of our lives, we feel well as whole beings. When we are living congruently, we smile more, are more focused and less distracted by all of the competing voices defining success in the world's terms.

When we are in touch with our inner wisdom, we face questions of congruence. We are clear about our values. We take the time to regularly consider the gap between what we say we believe and how we are acting. We regularly consider the fit between our own soul and the roles we are playing in our workplace, community and family. Wisdom is within us if we just take the time to access the treasures of our deepest knowing.

> We hang on to our values, even if they seem at times tarnished and worn; even if, as a nation and in our own lives, we have betrayed them more often than we care to remember. What else is there to guide us?
>
> **Barack Obama**

> We don't receive wisdom; we must discover it for ourselves after a journey that no one can take for us or spare us.
>
> **Marcel Proust**

Labyrinth at Grace Cathedral in San Francisco. In recent years, many people have rediscovered the importance of creating intentional time and space for silence and deep reflection on questions of congruence and values. Since 1991, Grace Cathedral has nurtured the use of the labyrinth walk for reflection, spiritual direction and healing with the guidance of Lauren Artress, one of the pioneers in exploring the applications of the labyrinth in our contemporary culture.

A diversity of ancient cultural and religious traditions speaks with a common voice about this wisdom that resides within each one of us. Whether we look at ancient Egypt or Africa or Babylonia, we find examples of proverbs, riddles and stories that are based on keen observation of humans and their environment, and reflect on what brings happiness and true fulfillment. At the heart of these wisdom writings in diverse cultures and historical periods is the recognition that wisdom comes from reflection on common human experience, not as some supernatural revelation to a select few. A key form this wisdom takes is the proverb, which is found in cultures around the world.

Proverbs offer maxims of common sense, understandable to anyone who stops to observe everyday life. For example, from the Hebrew book of Proverbs: "In the sin of his lips the evil man is ensnared, but the just comes free of trouble." (Proverbs 12:13) Numerous childhood fables and sayings portray the troubles that come from lies and untruths. The honest person doesn't have to worry about remembering the excuse he gave or whether or not an accomplice will tell the same story. A popular Brazilian proverb says, "The tree with the most leaves will not necessarily produce juicy fruit." The wise person knows that someone who says many words may not put those words into action. Simplicity and conciseness are often indicators of the ability to get the job done. Proverbs are very different from prophetic sayings or messages from an oracle. They do not rely on some transcendent or omniscient authority; rather they express what humans know from their experience and from simply paying attention to what is happening in the world. Behind these wisdom traditions from across the globe is a fundamental confidence in the human ability to see the truth that is embedded in reality.

Acting on the Authority of Interior Wisdom

The Jewish wisdom tradition tells stories of common, ordinary human beings who courageously stand up to power. One of the most interesting stories of such wisdom comes at the beginning of the book of Exodus. The Hebrews have become a threat to the Egyptians and, even though they are enslaved and forced to do endless manual labor, their numbers continue to grow. The story says that the Pharoah, who rules with divine authority, meets with the midwives Shiphrah and Puah and gives them the direct order to kill the Hebrew newborn boys. Instead, they act on their own wisdom as midwives; knowing the preciousness of life, they refuse to follow the dictates of the external authority. They don't have to consult the law or the priests. They know from their common human experience that newborn babies are meant for life, and they are willing to stand up to the highest authority in the land with their certain wisdom. Some commentators argue that these midwives were Egyptians themselves and still they refused to follow their pharaoh. They protect the lives of the newborn Hebrew boys even though they have been told that these children will grow to be a threat to their own existence. The midwives act in harmony with the natural process of life itself, with the fundamental wisdom that resides in reality and can be accessed by anyone who is willing to observe and reflect.

The wisdom traditions say that all informed, healthy persons have their own authority because each person has knowledge of what is right and good through intuition, observation and good reasoning. All persons have the authority to decide for themselves because they have the capability to figure out what is the wise thing to do. Authority for right action comes not from some external power but from interior wisdom. The search for this inner wisdom is not easy. It requires close attention to the experience of life, deep listening to the truth we know in our hearts, and openness to the dignity and value of all persons.

In the Christian scriptures, this wisdom from common human experience is seen in the parables of Jesus. When one lights a lamp one doesn't put it under a basket. When something very valuable is lost, one sweeps the whole house to find it. Seed that falls on good ground produces a hundredfold. The simple wisdom of soil, sheep, seeds and leaven are at the heart of the message of Jesus. Wisdom comes from close observation and clear thinking, recognizing the common natural consequences of one's words and actions.

The insight that the locus of wisdom is within us is also one of the fundamental teachings of the Buddha. Tradition has it that as the Buddha was dying, he advised his disciples, "Be a lamp unto yourself. Be your own confidence. Hold to the truth within yourself as to the only truth."[11] This isn't easy wisdom. It challenges us

> Inner wisdom is more important than wealth. The more you spend it, the more you gain.
>
> **Oprah Winfrey**

to deepen our reflection and our attentiveness. These profound wisdom traditions aren't saying we don't have to listen to experts or authorities. On the contrary, the messages from external authorities are only the beginning of wisdom. They must be reflected upon and considered in relationship to our deepest interior knowing. Often this kind of interior knowledge is called the knowledge of the heart. Carl Jung, the great explorer of the archetypes of human consciousness, said, "Your vision will become clear only when you look into your heart ... Who looks outside, dreams. Who looks inside, awakens."[12]

We are learning from the contemporary study of the brain, mind, body and emotions that we are integrated whole persons. The heart doesn't just pump blood, it knows things. Terms such as "heartache" or "heartbroken" hint at the knowing of the heart in constant connection with the brain and the rest of the body. Recent research reveals that the brain is really a distributed web of neurons throughout the body. Sometimes we can actually feel the knowing that comes from the nervous system that surrounds our stomachs when we have a gut reaction to an event or a story. Candace Pert's audio CD set *Your Body Is Your Subconscious Mind* explores the many dimensions of this research and its implications for practical wisdom.[13] Brain research also tells us that we can use the power of the mind to concentrate and focus attention to actually change the physical wiring of the brain. We can enlarge our physical brain capacity to be more empathic and compassionate through practice. Practical wisdom requires us to be attentive to the constant conversation of our body, heart, mind and spirit.

Ultimately, practical wisdom is a process, a way of living, not a destination. It isn't something we achieve but a way of being in conversation with our authentic, whole self. In the following chapters we describe one way of entering this conversation. We provide a laboratory and an experimental process for exploring personal wisdom, a safe space and method for investigating our deepest understanding. Practical wisdom requires a journey into our own stories, the internal geography of our spirits. In this space, on this journey, the distractions will fall away, the focus will both narrow and broaden, and our ears will become attuned to our own inner teacher. We will find all the wisdom we need. We will encounter the light within us that can outshine any darkness, the hope at our core that can sustain us through questions, doubts and difficulties.

We also provide some background information about the journey and the experiences of others who have used this laboratory. Some of us like to jump into the pool at the deep end, some of us like to test the water with a toe. The jumpers may wish to go straight to Chapter 4: Mountain 10 and start the climb to explore their own wisdom without any orientation from the guides. The toe testers may wish to read about the history and background for creating this way of practical wisdom. Either way, the journey beckons, the way of practical wisdom calls us to deeper joy, larger purpose, and a sense of peace and fulfillment, knowing that we are responding authentically to our unique call to embody this precious humanness.

Vision is not enough. It must be combined with venture. It is not enough to stare up the steps, we must step up the stairs.

Vaclav Havel

JOURNALING QUESTIONS

What are the places of strong fit in your life, where there is a clear connection between your activities, work, relationships and your core values, your soul? How does this "fit" bring you joy and purpose?

Where are the places of disconnect in your life? How does this disconnect affect your life?

How can you design space and time in your life for silence and reflection?

How would you define your mission in life?

What are your five most important values? In a sentence or two, describe each one.

What do you really want?

Chapter 2:
WISDOM TECHNOLOGIES ANCIENT AND NEW

The Mountain 10 technology is grounded in ancient traditions and pathways of wisdom, and accelerates the wisdom journey through its simplicity of design. It is critical to understand that wisdom is a journey, not a set of static principles or defined values. Although it is very important to articulate guiding principles and values for oneself or for one's organization, they are lifeless apart from their application in specific situations and concrete roles. The wise person or organization is in a constant process of discovery and renewal. This fundamental insight that wisdom is a process is communicated repeatedly in the great myths and wisdom practices of every culture. Mountain 10 includes a concentrated period of reflection--the climb to the summit--followed by a return down the mountain, and, finally, an extended process of guided integration. The integration process may lead to additional experiments in questioning and openness, in letting go and visioning. The pathway for the climb and the return is laid out in a LABgraphic, a map for the Mountain 10 journey. Before we look at the unique dimensions of the Mountain 10 technology, let us explore the several streams of wisdom that flow together in the creation of the new technology of Mountain 10.

One of these wisdom streams is the odyssey myth. Although in our modern usage myth is sometimes understood as a half-truth or fiction, our foundational myths present the most basic truths that give meaning, purpose and order to our lives. Often these fundamental myths are implicit and unconscious but they are the bedrock upon which our everyday considerations are based. They symbolically embody a worldview or a sense of reality out of which we live, an understanding of what is good, valuable and worthwhile. By offering a set of rich symbols and stories, myths provide a fundamental direction to life. They give rise to wisdom practices that are influenced by particular cultures and historical epochs. One of the most common myths embedded in cultures throughout the world is the foundational myth of the odyssey. Some of the key wisdom practices throughout the ages have emanated from this basic understanding of life. Mountain 10 is grounded in this timeless odyssey myth and combines ancient wisdom practices with new understandings from the fields of science, psychology and leadership studies.

The Odyssey Journey

The mythic pattern of the odyssey is evident across cultures and civilizations. The basic structure of this myth includes 1. the call to some great challenge, 2. an arduous journey to accomplish the heroic feat, and 3. the return home with new insight and understanding. In archetypal tales from every culture, a heroine or hero leaves home on a grand adventure to search for something that has been promised or lost, or to conquer some great evil. The journey often includes seemingly insurmountable hurdles, sometimes requiring the ascent of a perilous mountain peak or the descent into the underworld of the dead. The return home is usually even more dangerous than the quest.

The pattern of "call, journey, return" can be seen repeatedly in ancient folk tales as well as contemporary narratives in all forms of media because it is an "archetype" of human life. According to the Swiss psychiatrist Carl Jung, an archetype is an original pattern of thought or experience, a common form that is expressed across cultures and countries.[1] Films and novels that gain immense popularity often resonate with our own lives because they are based on these archetypes. The immensely popular *Jonathan Livingston Seagull* embodied this odyssey motif brilliantly.[2] Jonathan is cast out of his flock because he follows the higher purpose of flight. He believes flying is meant for more than simply catching fish. After a long journey of learning the highest forms of flying, he returns to his flock to lead them to freedom, to help them understand their true identity. The *Wizard of Oz* is another popular example of journeying in a strange land and coming to the insight that we are the wizards of our own lives.[3] We have within us all the wisdom, heart and courage that we need. The challenge is always to return home and put the insight into practice.

The most important thing to remember is this: to be ready at any moment to give up what you are for what you might become.Oprah Winfrey

W.E.B DuBois

PATTERN OF THE ODYSSEY MYTH

CALL	CALL to search for something important CALL to rescue someone in distress CALL to conquer some great evil
JOURNEY	JOURNEY to some great height JOURNEY to some great depth JOURNEY to new inner insight and wisdom
RETURN	RETURN to the place from which you left RETURN to home, now seen with new eyes

The Odyssey Pattern in Our Lives

This universal framework of transformation, call, journey, return, is experienced over and over in the rhythms of our own lives. A child is born into an awe-filled world that is largely unexplainable and uncontrollable. For months the child has no language to name the unknown and only through time and effort begins to learn categories that structure experience. Through cognitive and emotional development, the individual learns to get along in the world, to make a place of meaning and purpose, perhaps to find a job and a partner and create a home. In the final stages of life, there is usually a return to a sense of wonder and awe, not to the silence of being without words, but to the silence of knowing that words cannot exhaust the mystery. Many persons experience this pattern in important relationships which often begin with a call out of oneself into the unknown. Relationships are often experienced as adventures that take us away from home. The "other" presents a new world to explore, a new way of being. Over time, there is a return to being at home, but now with each other. In the best of relationships, this belonging includes a continual openness to the new.

The mythic odyssey pattern can also be seen in the process of adolescence which the famed child psychologist Erik Erikson termed individuation.[4] Adolescents flee from the constraints of their parents to explore the broader world outside of their families' attitudes and values. Sometimes there is significant rebellion against parental rules and expectations. However, if there is support and love, the process of exploration ultimately leads to a sense of self and the young adult "returns" to re-engage in the family with a greater level of maturity and self-awareness. Contemporary developmental theorists recognize that parents as well are going through a developmental journey along with their adolescent children. The parents' journey includes letting go of their children and trusting that they have learned the values and skills that they need. The empty nest may, at first, seem foreign and lifeless. However, through exploration, parents "return" to a home that provides the basis for renewed generativity that may take the form of volunteering, creative pursuits, and the joys of grandchildren.

A new job may be experienced as an odyssey journey that includes the call to lead or to learn new skills. There is a time of exploration and accelerated learning that is followed by settling again into a world of work that has a greater level of comfort, where one feels competent to meet the challenges of the role. All kinds of life experiences can be viewed from this framework of the odyssey journey, from going back to school for a new degree or certification to moving to a new home, from the seasonal process of gardening to the life-long process of personal development.

The wisdom process often begins with the experience of loss or the awareness of incompleteness. It may start with the question, "Is that all there is?" Wise persons pay attention to the persistent longings in their minds, bodies and spirits. They take time to consider what they are seeking. They ask themselves repeatedly, "What do I really want?"

There is hope in dreams, imagination, and in the courage of those who wish to make those dreams a reality.

Jonas Salk

The purpose of life is to live it, to taste experience to the utmost, to reach out eagerly and without fear for newer and richer experience.

Eleanor Roosevelt

WHAT ARE YOU SEEKING (by Gary Boelhower)

What are you seeking
to be of use a voice that matters
to be the wild
essence
of your individual question
the one that wakes you in the night
visits in the gut of your knowing

Listen then
bend to the earth
your ear to the voices of the children
to the suffering that runs
like untamed horses
stampede of need for water rice hope

Ten year old chained
to his work station stitching
soccer balls for fourteen hours
count the calluses on the hands
of the children
the empty eyes
bellies aching for bread
measure the continents
as they drift farther from each other
the galaxies
spinning deeper into space

Why are you waiting
grab on anywhere
find your own embrace and hold
on tight
kiss the wounds

The recognition of loss, emptiness or aridness initiates a process of questing and searching that culminates in new insight. It is not unusual for us to begin our exploration by seeking something external, a new job or a new home or a way to change our partner, and to find in the search an internal gift of new awareness that is much deeper and more precious than the answer we thought we were after. Often the odyssey journey is more about conquering one's internal fear than about slaying some dragon, more about accepting one's own genius than about finding a new infallible guru.

The Importance of the Return

The final step in the wisdom process is returning to one's life and putting the new awareness into practice. Upon our return, we often see with new eyes. Our vision has been enlarged or refocused. It is as if we are seeing our partner or our work or our children for the first time. T.S. Eliot expresses this experience powerfully when he says, "We shall not cease from exploration/And the end of all our exploring/Will be to arrive where we started/And know the place for the first time."[5] The return is an essential step in the wisdom process. Without the return, the journey is either an escape from responsibility or the curse of eternal exile. New ideas and creative urges leave us with a lot of loose ends unless they are woven into the tapestry of our lives. The "return" requires implementation, literally to realize a new vision, to make the possible real. When we return from our journey of exploration, we see with renewed perception and take the action steps to change our lives.

When we are deeply aware of this odyssey archetype we can recognize it in our own experience. We can be more attentive to the questions that arise, to the calls that we often hear from the needs of our communities and the urges of our own hearts. We can intentionally choose to set out on the journey and to deepen our exploration and questioning. We can allow the journey to teach us. We can take time to reflect on the insights that come from a careful consideration of the various valleys and mountaintops in our travels, in our lives. We can pay attention to the difficult process of integrating new insights into our everyday lives.

The three movements of the odyssey archetype--call, journey, return--are seen in many natural, cultural, and spiritual processes and practices. The process of the seasons presents the cyclical unfolding and enfolding of life, the natural movement that includes decay and renewal, seed and fruit, gathering resources into oneself and giving it all away. Parker Palmer in *Let Your Life Speak* calls our experience of the seasons a "wise metaphor for the movement of life.... The notion that our lives are like the eternal cycle of the seasons does not deny the struggle or the joy, the loss or the gain, the darkness or the light, but encourages us to embrace it all—and to find in all of it opportunities for growth."[6] This basic rhythm of life is a constant teacher for anyone who takes the time to listen. Every year we have the opportunity to reflect on our fruitfulness and what we are bringing to harvest, to consider what needs to lie fallow to prepare for future growth, to ask what new seeds of possibility need nurturing. The seasons remind us that the most fundamental story of hope and harvest, life and death, is the story of each of our precious lives.

It is not by muscle, speed or physical dexterity that great things are achieved, but by reflection, force of character, and judgment.

Marcus Tullius Cicero

Security is mostly superstition. It does not exist in nature, nor do the children of men as a whole experience it. Avoiding danger is not safer in the long run than outright exposure. Life is either a daring adventure, or nothing.

Helen Keller

The Pilgrimage Ancient and New

The odyssey archetype is embedded as well in the wisdom exercise of pilgrimage, which has been practiced throughout the ages. Some vacations are modern, secular equivalents of the pilgrimage experience, a special time of traveling to a dedicated place for renewal and reflection. Pilgrimage is a sacred event for many of the religions of the world. Buddhists travel to four major pilgrimage sites in India and Nepal, including Lumbini, the birthplace of Gautama Buddha and Bodh Gaya, the place of his enlightenment. There are descriptions of Christian pilgrimages as early as the fourth century to the "Holy Land" sites of Jesus' life, death and resurrection. The fifth pillar of Islam requires that all Muslims, who are able, make the "hajj," a sacred journey to Mecca, during their lifetime. Similarly, Hindus journey to Varanisi and Mathura for inspiration and reflection.

The pilgrimage to a sacred site or a vacation journey to an historical memorial or a location of natural beauty includes the process of leaving behind ordinary life and entering into a time and space set apart. There may be special prayers or conversations during the journey, and a pace and rhythm very different from one's usual routine. The journey culminates in an encounter with the sacred, the unknown or the beautiful. It is often an occasion for heightened reflection on one's purpose and direction in life. The pilgrim becomes connected to a community of fellow pilgrims and to the larger story of others who have followed this path. Always, there is the challenge of returning to one's regular life with renewed vitality, incorporating the insights of the journey or pilgrimage into the texture of everyday existence.

A prudent question is one half of wisdom.

Francis Bacon

Many early pilgrims made their journeys on foot; their pace provided time for reflection and often important conversation with their fellow pilgrims. For many people today, the act of walking is an intentional slowing down that involves a reflective rhythm or conversational attention. The award-winning American poet Edward Hirsch in his article "My Pace Provokes My Thoughts: Poetry and Walking" says,

> I love the leisurely amplitude, the spaciousness, of taking a walk... I
> love the sheer adventure of it...You cross a threshold and you're on
> your way. Time is suspended. ... Poetry is written from the body as
> well as the mind, and the rhythm and pace of a walk--the physical
> activity--can get you going and keep you grounded....walking seems
> to bring a different sort of alertness, an associative kind of thinking,
> a drifting state of mind."[7]

Hirsch alludes to the wisdom that comes through the body, specifically through the iterative or rhythmic activity of walking. Many poets, scientists and inventors have used walking as a way of letting the mind wander or opening themselves to the unconscious and the insights that can come from that storehouse of wisdom. The motion of walking is rhythmic like the waves of the ocean and joins us to the elemental forces of nature. Perhaps, this is why similar iterative movements, such as the motion of the cradle or the rocking chair can set us right, calm our stresses, and allow us to ponder and wonder.

Hirsch reminds us that "Walking takes us into the world but it also brings us home. We come back restored from nature or refreshed by the city. Sometimes we return depleted, sometimes elated."[8] The mythic "return" confronts us even in the everyday walk. Sometimes we come back with ideas that challenge us to action. Sometimes, we see a situation or an issue differently because we have taken a walk around the block. We return ready for a more open conversation with others in our life or with other possibilities in our own consciousness.

Vision Quest

Another wisdom practice that is shared by many indigenous cultures throughout the world is the vision quest. Often this is a rite of passage from childhood to adulthood. It is marked by three phases, very similar to the odyssey journey, which many anthropologists term separation, transition and reincorporation. A young person who is ready to take on the responsibilities of adulthood is separated from the community for a few days or weeks to receive their unique call. There may be special rituals that symbolize detachment from a person's previous role or status. Often, the initiate goes into the wilderness alone and is visited by a spirit animal or receives a vision indicating their unique purpose in the community. The final stage is one of return, re-entering society with a different standing or position, sometimes with a different name.

Today there are many organizations that provide vision quest experiences for those who are at a crossroads in life and wish to connect with the natural world as a means for renewing their vision. Individuals who choose to embark on a vision quest come from a broad variety of circumstances but generally have one thing in common—they hear a call to something more in their lives. Sometimes that call takes the form of burnout and frustration in work that no longer provides satisfaction. Sometimes the urge for something more comes after a major upheaval such as the loss of a job or spouse or failed business. From many walks of life, they come to the wilderness seeking transformation. Joseph Campbell, in his masterful exploration of cross-cultural myths *Hero with a Thousand Faces*, explains the experience of disillusionment that often leads one to seek a new vision. The familiar patterns, ideals and ways of thinking no longer seem fitting or life-giving. The experience of something new on the horizon, exciting and yet demanding, means there is a threshold to be crossed into a new adventure.[9] After a few days of preparation, individuals usually begin their quest with a symbolic crossing of the threshold into the wilderness, the liminal space of unknowing. There may be a prayer to the four directions, symbolizing the fullness of life and the openness to learning in all ways. Poised on the threshold, one takes a deep, cleansing breath. In the pause of the breath comes complete presence, totally inhabiting the body in space and time, fully aware of the step one is taking.

A very great vision is needed, and the man you has it must follow it as the eagle seeks the deepest blue of the sky.

Crazy Horse

Of course, it isn't necessary to go into the wilderness to enter into that transitional space. Some persons go on a retreat, start a journal, or join a support group. Some walk a sacred pathway as they consider an important question. Some draw a mandala or trace a spiral to help them meditate or center their attention. Some walk a labyrinth to let its turns and rhythms open an inner space for creativity or insight. Unlike a maze which includes confusing dead ends, the labyrinth is a clear circular pathway from the perimeter to the center and back out. There are labyrinths and spirals, medicine wheels and sacred pathways etched in cave walls, painted on canyon walls, and set in stone formations throughout the world. We might call them a family of ancient reflective technologies: tools for opening the imagination, for considering multiple perspectives, and for seeing one's life in a larger context of meaning.

Stone Labyrinth in Dritvik, Snaefellsnes, Iceland. Over 500 stone labyrinths can be found throughout the Nordic countries of Sweden, Norway and Finland and around the shorelines of the Baltic Sea. The many stone labyrinths in Iceland, arctic Russia and Estonia probably originated from Nordic settlers or trading contacts.

The Dialectical Process of the Labyrinth

One of the most effective technologies for internal exploration is the labyrinth. It affects the body, mind and spirit of a person through its clockwise and counterclockwise movement and repeated reorientation to one of the four directions. The repetitive, patterned movement of the labyrinth nurtures associative thinking and allows the wisdom of the unconscious to come out of hiding through images, metaphors and insights.

Labyrinth walkers often speak of revelations or epiphanies. Some talk of layers of an old self dissolving in the process of the walk. Others talk about their eyes being opened, things bubbling up, seeing from underneath, or seeing themselves from a far distance in relationship to a larger whole. Some speak of coming to a place of deep peace and balance. Some return to their lives and take courageous actions that they previously thought impossible.

The wisdom that can be gained from the labyrinth is evident in the many ways it has been a significant tool for deep reflection and action. Clare Wilson created the "reconciliation labyrinth" to work with people in South Africa healing from the experience of apartheid. It has two different entrances

> recognizing that as South Africans because of apartheid we do not start the journey toward reconciliation from the same place. … Sometimes the path allows us to travel alongside each other, sometimes it takes us away and sometimes towards each other but, if we keep walking, when we are at the furthest point from our divided entrance we find we are in the same path as each other. We then pass each other and walk the path that 'the other' has walked, gaining understanding along the way of how we were shaped to be where we are now.[10]

At Crossroads Elementary School in St. Paul, Minnesota, Susan Dustin, the school social worker, created a canvas labyrinth that students use for problem solving and conflict resolution.[11] As they walk the labyrinth, students talk about the conflict and their feelings, possible solutions and how they might find a way forward together. At the center of the labyrinth, they affirm each other. Dustin believes the labyrinth process is very beneficial because of its kinesthetic dimension. It has become a symbolic safe space for peace and understanding.

In many churches and retreat centers, the labyrinth is used in spiritual direction and reflection. At spas and wellness centers, it facilitates relaxation and mindfulness. At conferences and workshops on creativity and innovation, it helps individuals access their creative core. At over 200 hospitals, hospices and cancer centers, the labyrinth provides a place for healing and peace. It is also being used in prisons for deep reflection and integration. In organizations big and small, the labyrinth is used for team building, problem solving and visioning.

The eleven-circuit labyrinth (eleven courses around the center) in Chartres Cathedral, the most well-preserved and largest labyrinth from medieval times, is the pattern for Mountain 10. Although many of the ancient labyrinths have been destroyed and their origins and uses cannot be retrieved, scholars and explorers have discovered a great deal about the 11th-century Chartres school and the 13th-century Chartres labyrinth. The pattern and process of the labyrinth reveal one of the key principles of the Chartres school—that there is an understanding of the whole within which all particularities and differences are reconciled. The Chartres school embodied a new way of learning called "scholasticism" that included the seven liberal arts. Through dialectical reasoning and rigorous analysis, contradictions could be resolved and the ultimate harmony of the universe could be glimpsed. Human reason could penetrate the deepest mysteries. In the 11th century this was a radically new perspective. The complex geometrical design of the cathedral and its beautiful rose windows embody this sense of the power of human reason. If the west façade of the cathedral were to be folded inward, the great rose window would fall almost perfectly on the circle of the labyrinth.

CHARTRES (by Gary Boelhower)

They passed the code in secret
angle tangent intersect
circle rhombus square
the four directions cubed
and flung into the air
buttress pillar arch dome
reason number music dance
working in dream and stone
so the lofty rose window
light through the blue glass
and circle of the labyrinth
create one ringing center
one pulse in stone and song
so the heart opens
into fractal tessellations of fire.

The Labyrinth at Chartres Cathedral, Chartres, France. One of the best known labyrinths in the world, this beautifully-preserved labyrinth is set in the floor of Chartres Cathedral. It was constructed in the early 13th century and fills the nave of the cathedral.

The labyrinth walker moves in all directions, walks toward the center and away from the center, turns and turns again to see from multiple perspectives, moves clockwise and counterclockwise in the process of consideration and reconsideration. The labyrinth was an ancient technology for reflecting deeply on diverse viewpoints, listening to the truth of divergent voices, and seeing the larger truth and its interconnections.

Mountain 10: An Accelerated Process

Mountain 10 is an accelerated process based on the ancient technology of the labyrinth. It allows one to experience the patterned rhythm of labyrinth walking, the distinctive time of pilgrimage and vision quest, but doesn't require distant travels or a week in the wilderness. It connects us to the foundational myth of the odyssey journey as we explore inner geography that we may not have traversed before. Mountain 10 is not meant to replace other methods for reflection and insight. It is a unique wisdom practice in its own right. However, it participates in the motif of the odyssey because it involves both a journey into the unknown and the return home. It resembles the pilgrimage or vision quest because it requires time set aside to intentionally focus on what you are seeking. It uses the labyrinth form to create an iterative, rhythmic process of reflecting and questioning.

Mountain 10 uses the metaphor of mountain climbing because the journey to insight or creative resolution, whether individually or as a team or organization, is often difficult and involves a perilous journey. Frequently the way is steep and requires one well-placed step after another. We regularly run into assumptions or mental models that are boulders in our path. Sometimes our fears are gaping crevasses that seem too wide and deep to leap over. Finally, the mountain metaphor is connected to the idea of the world center, the "axis mundi." In virtually all cultures, there is a mythic place where heaven and earth meet. That place is usually a hill or mountain or pyramid. What we are seeking through the Mountain 10 technology is that place where things come together in an ultimate way, where there is a radical convergence of intuition and intellect. It is a place where we see from a higher perspective, from a new vantage point. We are able to see the whole and its interconnections. Mountain 10 is a way that leads us to a summit experience.

Mountain 10 is the result of many years of facilitating labyrinth experiences and reflecting on the uniqueness and effectiveness of this technology. Joe recalls his first labyrinth walk at a conference in Estes Park, Colorado in 1993:

> I walked the labyrinth with my eyes closed, holding hands with persons on both sides of me. It felt like walking on the edge of a mountain. Later, when I took the labyrinth into the Creative Problem Solving Institute, I remember feeling the rock and roll of it, the motion. I think I resonated with the rhythmic movement of the labyrinth because my father once held me in the Atlantic ocean when I was a young child. He always said that when the tide was high here it was low in his home country of Spain and when it was high tide in Spain it was low here. I grew up thinking of that motion and feeling being held in the ebb and flow of the ocean.

[In] the mythic tradition, the Mountain is the connection between Earth and Sky. Its highest summit touches the sphere of eternity, and its base branches out in manifold foothills into the world of mortals.

Rene Daumal

Since 1995, Joe and Tricia have guided labyrinth walks and retreats, facilitated workshops for conferences (e.g. Creative Problem Solving Institute, Center for Creative Leadership, Accelerated Learning Society) and corporations large and small (e.g. De Agostini Publishing, Era Energy, Dupont), using this ancient technology for problem solving, team development, strategic decision-making, organizational visioning and personal reflection.

Climbing to Our Own Summit

Mountain 10 allows anyone anywhere to enter a unique, dangerously-safe space where we are guided to climb to our own summit of exploration. The iterative rhythm of Mountain 10 allows the body's wisdom to find a voice as we imaginatively turn again and again to enter other dimensions of our expanding awareness. A process of carefully orchestrated questions deepens our consideration and opens our mind to the challenges that we face at the level of identity and ultimate purpose. The pattern of the Mountain 10 climb ignites the human imagination so that pictures, feelings, and images arise from both the unconscious and conscious memory to fuel our personal insights. The paradoxical safety and risk of Mountain 10 allows us to be in the space of not knowing so that we can let go of our comfortable assumptions and habitual mental models.

> We do not need magic to transform our world. We carry all the power we need inside ourselves already. We have the power to imagine better.
>
> **J.K. Rowling**

Because it is an iterative process in a safe but challenging space, Mountain 10 is an emergent technology. In other words, it facilitates the emergence of memories and insights, past images and new dreams. It encourages wonder, association, leaps in understanding, seeing connections and intersections. Often participants remark, "This memory bubbled up from my past." or "This insight came up." People using Mountain 10 for problem solving or innovation have remarked "This vision emerged out of the mist." and "Pieces of the puzzle kept floating to the surface."

Critical to any laboratory space is the act of observing. All great insights begin with seeing, becoming aware of what is really there. For the Mountain 10 climber the terrain is interior—emotions, images, previous explanations, and patterns of behavior. When we begin to see the possibility of something new, we are faced with the challenge of letting go of the old. Real growth requires shedding the old skin or leaving the shell that has become too small for our dreams. The Mountain 10 journey switches back and forth, gains ground and loses ground, meanders a pathway that keeps asking the important questions. Often it isn't until the fourth or fifth answer to "why" that we get to the real reasons. Our first observations are obvious but, as we are challenged to look more deeply, we begin to see roadblocks and possibilities that we didn't see before.

> Hold fast to dreams,
> For if dreams die
> Life is a broken-
> winged bird
> That cannot fly
>
> **Langston Hughes**

Mountain 10 is not the name of the summit, but rather identifies a point in the climb close to the summit that is a natural decision point. Mountain climbing stories often focus on the summit but climbers know there is a long, arduous process over many peaks and valleys before the summit is attempted. As the climb gains altitude and difficulty and the climbers grow weary, there comes a point where a decision must be made. Knowing the difficulty and risks of this mountain and its environment, do we go on or do we turn back? Tricia and Joe observed themselves and hundreds of other participants intuitively stopping at the tenth critical turn in the labyrinth. It is a unique marker in the journey, where there is a deep awareness of both the path already traveled and the remaining challenges to reach the summit that can be glimpsed in the distance. Tricia tells of a powerful experience of being frozen in this spot for nearly an hour, aware of all that she would need to let go of in order to enter a new vision for her life, somehow knowing that the next step, if she took it, would start a process of major transformation.

Participating at a Labyrinth Gathering, held at Omega, Rhinebeck, New York, in 1995, Tricia decided to walk the labyrinth one evening. A multitude of votive candles around the outer rim of the labyrinth illuminated the beauty of the site. It was a dark, crisp night. Tricia approached the entrance of the labyrinth and gazed at the serenity of the space. She set an intention for the walk, took a deep cleansing breath, and stood between the markers of the entrance.

The walk proceeded as a slow, contemplative journey, as it had in past experiences. Tricia was keenly aware of her passage through the quadrants of the labyrinth, moving through turns that would not be repeated until she was on the return from the center. As she moved into the third quadrant (the Vision quadrant), she sensed she was approaching a critical turning point. She was aware of a palpable energy in her body and in the air surrounding her. She stopped in the tenth turn of the labyrinth path and stood there--still, balanced, erect and tall--for nearly an hour. Her arms hung beside her torso, palms facing front. (She later discovered that this stance is the Yoga pose, tadasana, meaning mountain.) She seemed to be suspended in time and space, comfortable and challenged at the same time. Tricia looked back at the labyrinth pattern to count the turns she had made. She wanted to be able to remember the location of this incredible event--turn ten in the Vision quadrant. This was a unique point in the journey, a point where the past and present gathered at a new threshold of possibility. She realized one choice was to turn around and leave the labyrinth without completing the journey. Metaphorically, it would mean choosing a continuation of her current life direction. The other choice would be to move on through the Vision quadrant and step into the fourth quadrant of Realization.

UNRAVELING LIGHT: A LABYRINTH JOURNEY (by Tricia Pearce)

Do I dare wonder
Where the wandering goes?

It's dark
And Light is but a longing.

Songs move the wind,
But, I can't taste them.

Feelings flash like fireflies,
I dare not hold them.

I know without understanding.
I can dance this.

I must risk
Unraveling into the Light.

It's time to journey Home!

In her mind, Tricia could see herself making the choice, finalizing the Vision quadrant and moving to grasp her intention as reality. She knew this was the only way to attain the change she sought. This experience of being frozen in the tenth turn of the labyrinth was the beginning of Mountain 10. After much observation and research, it became clear that the tenth turn was an archetypal movement. Ancient calendars and numerical symbols relate the number ten to completeness, to a decision point where there is both ending and beginning. Based on the experience of many participants at this important juncture in the labyrinth and further study of its archetypal connections, Mountain 10 provides an intentional questioning process at this point in the journey, a decision point that gives participants the opportunity to more fully understand their own attachments to the past and the risks and opportunities of the future.

The Mountain 10 technology will guide you to the summit but the way will move through deep awareness, letting go, visioning, and making the vision real in your life. Every climber makes their own way, at their own pace. Mountain 10 is the climb of your life, your story, your own internal wisdom.

When you participate in the Mountain 10 process, you aren't getting someone else's answer or someone else's advice. You are listening to your own wisdom that speaks in the still small voice of your heart's deepest longing. Mountain 10 is a technology with simple design and intense content that helps you recover your internal, holistic intelligence that brings together body, mind and spirit; reason and

Stories are the creative conversion of life itself into a more powerful, clearer, more meaningful experience. They are the currency of human contact.

Robert McKee

faith; science and intuition. Most techniques for reflection and decision-making tend to offer recipes and toolboxes. They often provide seven steps to the perfect body, the fulfilling relationship, the satisfying job, or the wonderful life. Mountain 10 helps you enter the depths of your own story and what it can teach you. This is the pathway that leads into the inner recesses of your deepest knowing, where you can gain clarity, a sense of your own internal compass, and raw honesty with yourself.

JOURNALING QUESTIONS

Reflect on the last time you "went into the wilderness." Why did you go? What did you find? What happened on your return?

What is the foundational story or myth of your life? Are there elements of this story that aren't working for you? How are you being drawn to rewrite the story as you move forward?

Reflect on three key peak or mountain-top exhilarating experiences. What did you learn about yourself from each of these experiences? What are the common threads that connect these three experiences?

Reflect on three dry, desert experiences. What got you through the most dry and dark times? What enabled you to go on? What did you learn about yourself from each of these experiences?

Chapter 3:
PREPARING FOR MOUNTAIN 10.

To prepare for the Mountain 10 climb, you won't need to learn knots, monitor weather systems or tone your leg muscles. However, you will need to create time and space for your individual exploration, for your climb to the summit of your own possibility. Although physical strength and stamina will not be required, your personal authenticity and perseverance will be put to the test. The experience will ask you to be clear and honest with yourself, to examine your shadows and your wounds, to stand in the brightness of your own genius and talents. You will explore the geography of your internal world so you might function at your full potential in your external world.

If you have done some of the journaling suggested in chapters one and two, you have already begun your interior preparations. The minimum amount of time needed to complete Mountain 10 is one hour. You may move through the process more slowly or quickly, depending on your own pace, questions, and depth of exploration. If you can set aside ninety minutes, you should have enough time to do some important journaling after the experience.

Find a sanctuary space as suggested in chapter one, a bright clearing for personal exploration, a place where you can plant your *heart* "like the seed of everything possible, everything to hope for, to believe in."[1] Choose a private, safe and special place where you can focus on your own wisdom and listen deeply to your own calling. It should be a place where you will not be interrupted and where you are free to feel deeply.

Feelings of various kinds may arise as you make your journey. You may experience sadness as you reflect on betrayals, recall losses, or confront the internal demand to let go of hurts or grudges from the past. Hopelessness and doubt may come rushing in as you turn a corner on your mountain climb and run into internal roadblocks, hurdles or wounds that stop you in your tracks. Exhilarating feelings of new possibility and gratitude may wash over you and revitalize you. Hope and confidence may grow as you settle into the repetitive rhythm of the climb. These and hundreds of other constellations of feelings have been reported by those who have traversed the Mountain 10 process before you. All have returned from the journey with new insight and wisdom.

The last step depends on the first. Don't think you have arrived just because you see the peak. Watch your feet, be certain of your next step, but don't let this distract you from the *highest* goal. The first step depends on the last.

René Daumal

The LABgraphic and Its Four Quadrants

We differ, blind and seeing, one from another, not in our senses, but in the use we make of them, in the imagination and courage with which we seek wisdom beyond the senses.

Helen Keller

To prepare for your Mountain 10 climb acquaint yourself with the LABgraphic on page 51. The LABgraphic is a map for your Mountain 10 journey and provides a clear pathway that leads to the summit of the mountain, the center of this laboratory space. Along the path, there are waypoints or markers that provide opportunities for reflection on your journey. The LABgraphic is divided into four quadrants or terrains: the *Awareness* quadrant, the *Letting Go* quadrant, the *Vision* quadrant and the *Realization* quadrant. In our work with hundreds of participants through the years, we have found that these quadrants name important dimensions of the human change process. We do not see the need to change until we become aware of our discomfort or pain, or until we are gripped by a challenge or possibility that demands our attention. Sometimes, we simply recognize that there is a gap between what we are doing presently and what we really want to be doing, between who we are now and who we really want to be. This awareness motivates us to consider what we need to let go of.

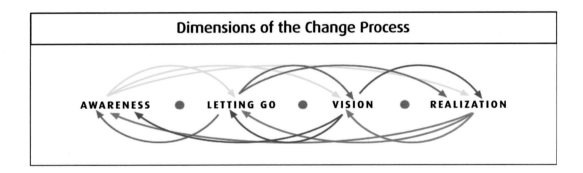

Dimensions of the Change Process

AWARENESS   LETTING GO   VISION   REALIZATION

For many letting go is the most difficult part of the journey of change. Our present state is grounded in a set of habitual ways of thinking and acting. We've grown used to this way of being and doing; we take it for granted. In the *Letting Go* quadrant we begin to see how our customary thoughts and actions haven't been serving us well. The old story we've been telling ourselves keeps us stuck in patterns that prevent our optimal growth. Letting go requires that we shed our old skin. This is a process that leaves us vulnerable, raw, and unprotected. As we let go, pieces of old patterns fall away. We find ourselves in a new land that is unknown and unexplored. We are poised at the frontier of our possibilities, in an unmapped land full of danger and promise. Here, on the threshold, we are challenged to embrace our vision.

The *Vision* quadrant invites us to see with new eyes, to tell a new story. In this quadrant, we begin to put words and images to the dream that has been gestating in our hearts. Sometimes the vision comes as a different feeling about life. Sometimes it comes as a mental picture of new work, new home, or new self. Sometimes, it comes as a statement of purpose and goals. In the *Vision* quadrant, the possible begins to emerge.

As we move into the *Realization* quadrant, we begin to put concrete steps to our new vision. We begin to translate the possible into definite actions. If the *Vision* quadrant invites us to take a leap of faith, the *Realization* quadrant converts that leap into real, doable deeds. In this quadrant we get down to the nitty-gritty details of the change process. If we have been authentic in our awareness, letting go and vision processes, realization is both simple and complex, easy and difficult. To realize the new vision takes time, thoughtfulness, and planning. If we have the courage to feel the pull of possibility, we will have the motivation to change.

The Mountain 10 climb is not a straight, linear path. It switches back and forth so that our ascent is gradual and achievable. Therefore, we will revisit each of the quadrants of the LABgraphic several times. In a sense, these quadrants are like the different terrains that a climber moves through on the way to the summit. There are no sharp demarcation lines between one terrain and another. In the *Awareness* quadrant, we awaken to deeper questions, feelings in our bodies, images in our minds. We pay attention to what is arising, to what is emerging within us without judging or analyzing. We become aware of our awareness. We recognize how we are the witnesses to every moment of our lives. We broaden our focus to see the big picture, the patterns and rhythms of our life, the seasons and turning points. We narrow our focus to the single breath, the single heartbeat, the smallest cell of our experience, knowing that each moment is a hologram that contains our whole life. We will return to this quadrant three times. Each time we move into this terrain, we are asked to simply notice what is happening, to observe ourselves in the process of the climb. Each time, we ask: What am I feeling in my body? What is arising in my heart and mind? What am I observing outside and inside?

In the *Letting Go* quadrant, we are asked to surrender. We begin to let go of baggage and burdens that weigh us down. We discard our old mental models that have become too small for our hopes and yearnings. We jettison the expectations of others that have trapped us in a vision that is not our own. Like hermit crabs that outgrow their shells, we move out of our old structures and meanings to find a more spacious place. There is grief and emptiness in letting go. We say goodbye to the familiar and safe, and greet the dawn of something unknown. We live in the paradox of expectation and fear, excitement and dread. We silence the voices that call us back to the tried and true, urging us to be cautious, counseling us to play it safe. We stop believing those who would diminish us. Our journey will cycle through this quadrant four times. Each time we move into this terrain, we are asked to let go of our small visions and safe dreams. Each time, we ask: What is no longer serving my best self? What is holding me back? What must I leave behind to walk into the vision that is waiting for me? Some of us may choose courageously to give up comfortable patterns, commitments and relationships that prevent us from listening to the new song that is beginning to rise in our hearts and lungs.

It's not the load that breaks you down, it's the way you carry it.

Lena Horne

Don't ask what the world needs. Ask what makes you come alive, and go do it. Because what the world needs is people who have come alive.

Howard Thurman

Give us clear vision
that we may know
where to stand and
what to stand for—
because unless we
stand for something
we shall fall for
anything.

Peter Marshall

As we enter the *Vision* quadrant, we receive hints and glimpses of what is possible in our lives. We open ourselves to the creative urge that is calling from within. Sometimes our new vision is something we have known all along but we now have the courage to embrace it. Some are struck with a radical revelation that seems to come from out of the blue and yet feels right. In this quadrant, it is as if we are seeing with new eyes. There is a sense of clarity about the way forward. It will not necessarily seem easy or painless, but it will seem possible. For many, there will be an undeniable insistence about this new vision. As we return to this quadrant four times in the journey, we will see the way opening more clearly before us. Each time we ask: What is the lure of possibility in my life? What creative urge is calling within? What is the shape of the promise emerging from the mist up ahead?

The final terrain of our journey is the *Realization* quadrant. Here we begin to see how to bring our vision into reality. We literally recognize the steps or dimensions of making the possible real, shaping it in the concrete circumstances of our lives. We will visit this realization quadrant three times. Each time we move into this terrain we will identify specific actions or decisions that will bring our new vision alive. We ask: What is one of the most important actions I can take to move in the direction of my dream? To whom can I tell this new story and how will I ask them to help me live it?

Although the four quadrants seem to be delineated separately in the LABgraphic, thinking of them as terrains helps us understand how these aspects of the journey meld into each other. When we begin to see from these four directions or four perspectives we become oriented to our whole humanness, to the wonderful, diverse dimensions of our internal geography. The terrains flow out of and into each other.

Waypoints on the Journey

The waypoints or checkpoints throughout the LABgraphic mark our progress on the journey. You may wish to pause briefly at these points and focus on the work of the quadrant that you are in, the particular questions of this terrain. Go at your own pace, whatever feels right for your unique journey. The tenth waypoint is Mountain 10, a high point from which you can reflect on your journey so far, but not the end of the climb. Mountain 10 is a decision point. It gives us the opportunity to consider: Am I willing to go forward, to live into my vision, to do what my dream will require of me? Should I turn back or go for the summit? Since this is a very important juncture on the journey, you are asked to pause and deeply reflect at this key point. The last leg of the climb to the summit must be done with intention and care. In an age of risk management and risk aversion, it is important to take the time to gain clarity about what you really want at the Mountain 10 waypoint. Do you want it enough to take the final risk?

Getting to the top
is optional. Getting
down is mandatory.

Ed Viesturs

Hikers Make the Long Trek in to Mount Hood. Mountain 10 is not the summit but a high place from which the way already traversed and the rest of the way to the summit can be seen. It is a decision-point in the journey. What have I learned from this journey and do I commit to making the rest of the climb?

Ultimately, our climb takes us to the summit—the high place from which we can see in all directions. As we arrive in the center of the LABgraphic, we take three deep breaths to bring ourselves into the full presence of this moment at the apex of our journey. From this axis mundi, this center point of the world of our lives, we are able to celebrate our new awareness, to honor our willingness to shed the baggage that does not serve us, to appreciate our new vision, and to look forward to the full realization of our dream. We may experience a sense of profound stillness and peace at the center of the LABgraphic but our time on the summit is brief. We have only made half the journey. Now, we must journey back and return to our everyday lives. Our journey out of the center or down from the summit must be measured and intentional. Although the climber coming down is being pulled by gravity, the way can be hazardous if done too quickly. We are challenged to integrate our new knowledge with the ordinary activities of our occupation and personal lives. The wisdom of the climber must be turned into actions and attitudes in our families and workplaces. The rapt attention of the climber must be translated into living more deeply present to our fellow workers, friends, and relations. The real journey is the return, to put into practice the treasured insights we found on the climb, to live with the grand perspective that we saw from the summit.

For our first Mountain 10 climb in the next chapter, we will trace the path of the LABgraphic with two colors, red and blue. We recommend a red and blue Crayola crayon. The feel of crayons on paper and the smell of their waxy colors may help us enter into the experience with childhood exploration, with a curious mind and an open heart. We use red and blue because they are far apart in the human visible spectrum of color. The human eye sees three basic colors: red, green and blue based on the three types of cone receptors at the back of the eye. Red has a long wavelength and low frequency; blue has a short wavelength and high frequency. These two colors represent the challenge of the Mountain 10 journey from letting go of the old to envisioning the new. We will color in the path of the LABgraphic with the red crayon for much of our first Mountain 10 climb since the process of letting go is a difficult and critical step before we can begin to write a new story of possibility for ourselves. Red symbolizes the letting go process of emotional release, freeing our selves from unrealistic expectations and false identities. We use the blue crayon to color in the waypoints on the LABgraphic to symbolize that our vision emerges from our journey. We slowly learn to see and express our brightest potential as we move back and forth through the terrains of our inner geography. On the last part of the Mountain 10 journey, we will switch to the blue crayon to color in our path. Blue symbolizes that our vision is becoming clearer as we embrace the boldest possibilities for our lives.

Colors have many meanings and associations that differ from one person to another based on individual experiences and cultural traditions. Often we have an intuitive response to colors. For many red and blue represent the poles of passion and reason, the strength of emotion and the clarity of intellect. In the ancient chakra energy systems of Hinduism and Buddhism, red is associated with the root chakra at the base of the spine. This is the chakra of survival, our identity and our physical connection to the universe. Blue is associated with the throat chakra which is the energy of speech and expression. On our Mountain 10 journey we become more fully aware of our gifts and talents and the obstacles to their full expression. We listen deeply to the call within and begin to see how we might embody the boldest vision for our lives. The colors of red and blue represent this movement from internal recognition to external realization. We let go of what is getting in the way of living the fullness of our potential, the boldness of our dream. We begin to express our vision in new attitudes and actions.

The Importance of Intention

Before we begin our journey, we must set a personal intention. What do you really want? Go inside, listen to your heart speak its deepest truth. This intention will guide you throughout your climb. Each step along the path will reflect this deep desire. You will see your dream from many perspectives. You will consider what it requires from you and what it promises for you. Before you cross the threshold onto your personal path of exploration, try to be as clear as you can be about your intention, about what you really want. You will press your finger on the entrance to the LABgraphic path, feeling your full presence and anchoring your intention.

It is not unusual for a person's intention to change during the Mountain 10 climb. We are faced with a paradox--be clear about your intention and yet not too attached to it. Carry your highest dream into this safe and dangerous space of exploration and let the journey itself teach you about your deepest desire. Let the way open before you. When your intention is clear, you will take one deep breath, cross the threshold, and enter the path.

The Mountain 10 process is not about the mountain; it's about the climb, your climb and your experience. Make the journey your own. Although we provide directions and waypoints and questions, focus on what serves you. Mountain 10 is an emergent technology, a tool, not an end. It is a means to help you explore your own inner wisdom. Focus less on the directions than on the direction your heart is pulling you. Focus less on the questions provided than on the question that is echoing in the chambers of your heart. Focus less on the external path than on the way that opens within. There aren't any wrong turns. There isn't any right speed. The Mountain 10 technology is a dangerously safe laboratory; you are the experiment and the researcher.

MOVING THROUGH THE LABYRINTH (by Tricia Pearce)

the rock
of the
body,

the sweep
of the eye
across
the landscape

connecting
past, present
and future

Our intention creates our reality.

Wayne Dwyer

After you have completed the journey to the summit and the return down the mountain, it is important to spend a minimum of ten minutes in reflection and journaling. We will provide five final questions to help you anchor your experience and insights. Your responses will help you identify your most important learning from your Mountain 10 journey. Take the time you need to reflect on your transition back into ordinary life. You will be called in extraordinary ways to continue the climb to full realization of what you really want.

The process of integrating your insights from the Mountain 10 climb may be challenging. It may take several months to shape the life that revealed itself in your vision. The final chapter of this book is dedicated to maximizing the integration of your Mountain 10 journey, writing your new story in actions and attitudes. You can intentionally deepen your learning and integration through regular reflective practices. It is helpful to return to your responses to the final questions of the Mountain 10 experience. We call this "working the questions." It allows you to revisit your climb, re-engage with the energy and emotion of your insights, and open yourself to what life is teaching you about your vision.

As you work on the integration process, translating your vision into decisions that serve your best possibilities, it may be helpful to experience Mountain 10 again. Many people use Mountain 10 as a regular reflective practice. Some use it as they face important decisions or choice points. Some use it as a problem-solving tool, others as an innovative thinking tool. No two Mountain 10 climbs are the same. Even if you enter the LABgraphic with the same intention as before, the process may expand and deepen for you. Your present mood and the immediate experiences of the day will influence your journey. Because you have changed, your journey will change. If you are open, the four terrains of awareness, letting go, vision and realization will give up new insights. You may wish to focus on your original intention or you may bring new questions or yearnings into the journey.

Whether you are climbing Mountain 10 the first time or the twelfth time, be clear about your intention before you enter the LABgraphic. Then move at your own pace, focusing on your internal geography and following the guidance of your intuition. Take time to be aware of the quadrants as you enter and leave them. Listen to the questions that arise in each terrain. What are you observing? What do you need to let go? What is your vision of the possible? What are the steps that will bring your vision into reality? Take time to reflect on the questions at the tenth waypoint, Mountain 10, and again after you return from the summit. The following questions may help you make your final preparations for the climb.

At the center of your being you know who you are. You know what you want.

Lao Tsu

JOURNALING QUESTIONS

What excites you? Explore the source of this reaction.

What makes you run away? Explore the source of this reaction.

Bring to mind an important wisdom figure in your life, someone you respect deeply. If you could ask this person one question, what question would you ask? How might they answer?

If you had to choose only three values as the bedrock or foundation for your life, what three values would you choose? Write a brief description of each of these values.

Name three of your most significant achievements in your personal or professional life. What do these achievements reveal about who you are?

What are three of the happiest moments of your childhood? What are three of the most difficult moments of your childhood? How have these moments continued to affect your life?

If you were granted three wishes without any strings attached, what would your three wishes be?

Chapter 4:
MOUNTAIN 10.

The Calling

Welcome to Mountain 10. This experience is an opportunity for you to enter your own story, to see its challenges and successes, its deep valleys of doubt and its mountaintops of achievement. As you walk the way of practical wisdom intentionally, you will meet your own inner teacher, the wisdom that lives within you. Although you will be navigating a path on a flat circular surface, for the purposes of this experience, you might think of yourself as a climber seeking the summit. As with all seekers, you will need to engage your skills of attention and observation, carefully and intentionally making your way.

The Way

The way mapped out for you is an ancient path that is surprisingly ever new. You will be following the way of pilgrims and philosophers, mountain climbers and pioneers, wanderers and wayfarers, monks and mystics. This journey has been mapped out in mandalas, labyrinths and pathways for centuries. All of its various forms from every culture and epic in history have had one purpose—to help those who journey find their way, not in the external geography of ordinary travel but in the internal geography of discovery, vision and purpose.

The Mountain 10 journey uses a LABgraphic based on the 13th-century labyrinth laid in the floor of Chartres Cathedral in Chartres, France. It will take you along a path that has been well worn but is new to your particular way of stepping and searching. It is called a LABgraphic because it is a laboratory space intentionally created for your experimentation, testing your own wisdom, for observing and listening to yourself. As you enter the LABgraphic, you cross a threshold and enter your own story.

What is the story you've been living? What is the story you've been telling yourself? Are there parts of your story that have brought deep joy and clear satisfaction? How do you continue to build on those aspects of your story? Are there parts of your story that have brought a sense of dissonance or have harmed your spirit? How might you change those aspects of your story? We often create habitual patterns over time—ways we think about ourselves or treat ourselves, ways we interact with our family and friends, ways we engage or disengage at work. These habitual patterns often become a central framework for our story. Sometimes these patterns become so ingrained in our everyday lives that we begin to think of ourselves as a character in the story rather than the author of our own lives. We become imprisoned in our own story when we actually hold the key within our own hands.

We have the opportunity to write the story of our future. We need not repeat the past. Of course, we are not in control of everything. However, we can control our vision, intention and attitude. We can take decisive action to change aspects of our story that aren't serving us well.

Tracing your way along the LABgraphic, you will climb to Mountain 10, a choice point, and then on to the summit. You will journey back and forth through four different terrains or quadrants of the circle: Awareness, Letting Go, Vision, and Realization. The way up a mountain is never straight. The LABgraphic path is recursive and involves the iterative process of switching back and forth. Every mountain has its own rhythm and so does every climber.

You will make your way down the mountain with a new awareness, having seen things from above, having felt the challenges and difficulties of the climb. This path will help you find your way to your own deepest wisdom. You may see key elements of your own story and patterns in your life with more clarity. You will be able to consider the new story you may wish to create as you step back into the world with new insight.

The Power of Intention

The outcome of this experience is highly dependent upon your intention or purpose. Wisdom will come to you if you intend to receive it, if you are clear about the question, issue or challenge you are facing. The most important question is "What do you really want?" What's in your heart? There are many distractions that call for our energy and commitment. Our stories may contain examples of seeking things that did not bring us joy. Now is the time to focus on what matters. What do you really want? Only you can answer that question. Intention is the energy behind the manifestation of your vision.

As you are about to begin your journey, take time to quiet yourself and reflect; then write down your intention.

What do you really want?

Tools

Ropes, anchors, stoppers and cams are NOT the tools you will need for this climb. You will need silence—a minimum of one uninterrupted hour of precious time. You will need intention, crystal clear intention, about what you really want. You will need focus, attention to how you are feeling and awareness of what you are thinking on the way. There will be many distractions but with focus you will return again and again to your clear intention and what you are learning from yourself. You will need openness—the willingness to let the new into your consciousness, to not judge a new thought or feeling or intuition harshly, and to see the profound wisdom at the core of who you are. **Finally, you will need a red and blue crayon.** Follow the directions carefully.

DIRECTIONS FOR THE JOURNEY:

- Take several breaths to settle yourself for the task at hand. Pay attention to your feeling, thinking, seeing and hearing (inner and outer voice). Bring your intention clearly to your mind and heart. Hold close the intention you have written to the question "What do you really want?"

- Press the tip of your forefinger on the waypoint or circle at the entrance to the LABgraphic path on the following page. Let go of your expectations. Experience your pulse, anchor your intention. Notice where you are and remember who you are. Take one deep breath, recall your intention. Using the RED crayon, enter the path.

- You are crossing the threshold into your interior adventure. Move through the AWARENESS quadrant into the LETTING GO quadrant. Fully color in the path as you go until you reach the first waypoint or circle on the path which is in the LETTING GO quadrant.

- Color the waypoint BLUE. You may want to write down what you are thinking or feeling about your INTENTION in this LETTING GO quadrant or terrain. A sheet of paper with the four quadrants (Mountain 10 Quadrant Reflections, page 59) is provided for you if you wish to jot down thoughts and feelings as you move through the terrains of the LABgraphic.

- Switching back to the RED crayon, continue following the path and fully coloring it in as you go. Pay attention when you re-enter the AWARENESS quadrant. Follow and color in the path until arriving at the second waypoint. Color the waypoint BLUE. You may want to write down what you are thinking or feeling about your INTENTION in this AWARENESS quadrant.

- Switch back to the RED crayon and fully color in the path as you go. Notice as you move into and out of a new quadrant. Use the BLUE crayon to color in the waypoints. You may want to write down what you are thinking or feeling about your intention at each of the waypoints, being aware of the quadrant in which you are climbing. Go at your own pace, find your own rhythm. Be aware of what you are noticing, hearing, feeling.

- Continue this process until you reach the tenth waypoint, Mountain 10, which is marked with a red waypoint. At this point, STOP. Put the crayons aside and look at your journey. Reflect on the questions on page 52 (Questions at Mountain 10 Waypoint: Writing Your Own Story), jotting down your answers if you wish.

MOUNTAIN 10 . LABgraphic

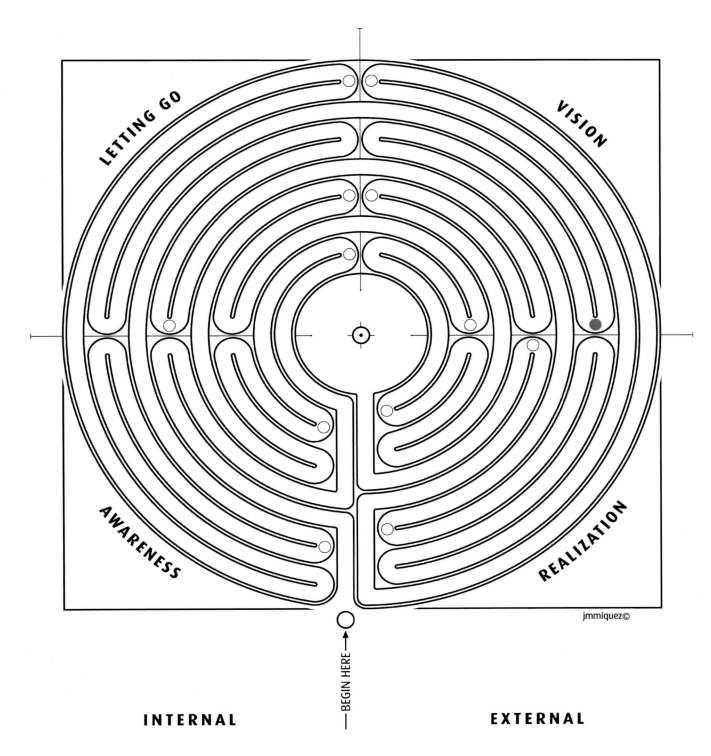

jmmiquez©

INTERNAL

EXTERNAL

Questions at Mountain 10 Waypoint: Writing Your Own Story

What did you see or notice during your climb so far? (Notice how far you've come. Pay attention to what is colored in and what is yet to come. Look at the LABgraphic from different points of view, turning the book to provide multiple perspectives.)

What were you feeling during your climb? What are you feeling now?

What were you thinking during your climb? What are you thinking now?

What happened? Did you experience anything unexpected?

What insights do you have now?

- After you have considered the Questions at Mountain 10 Waypoint, use the BLUE crayon to color in the rest of the path to the summit, again being aware of the quadrants through which you are moving. If you wish, jot down any thoughts and feelings as they occur in this final part of the climb to the summit.

- Make your way to the CENTER of the LABgraphic, to the higher ground from which you can see the whole. Place your forefinger on the center of the summit, feel your pulse, notice where you are and who you are. Take three deep breaths. Rest here, take a few minutes to be grateful for the journey, to appreciate your own story.

- THE RETURN: Ultimately the Mountain 10 experience is about the return—returning home with the gifts and insights of the journey. Now with your finger, trace your way through the LABgraphic, down the mountain, remembering your journey, being aware of the quadrants which you are passing through again. Be careful to move with attention and intention. Don't let the gravity of the down-hill journey rush you. Can you take the wisdom you have touched and bring it back home? What is required for you to make your new story come alive? Going down the mountain may be more difficult than the climb up. Be careful with each step. Hold on to your intention as you descend the mountain. Remember, it is about the return.

- When you arrive at the entrance to the LABgraphic, stop. Be fully present, take three deep breaths and be conscious about taking your first step back into your everyday reality. The climb is over AND it is just beginning. Revisit the intention you wrote down on page 49. Now, what do you really want?

- Take a few minutes to answer the Mountain 10 Final Reflection Questions on pages 54-58. Jot down the date you complete each answer so you can keep track of your different responses as you continue to reflect on these questions through the integration process.

Mountain 10 Final Reflection Questions

1. WHAT NO LONGER BRINGS YOU JOY OR TAKES YOU AWAY FROM YOUR SOURCE? WHAT DO YOU CHOOSE TO LET GO?

2. **WHAT BRINGS YOU JOY AND IS IN ALIGNMENT WITH YOUR SOURCE?
    WHAT DO YOU CHOOSE TO KEEP?**

3. WHAT DO YOU CHOOSE TO ADD TO KEEP YOUR SOURCE FUELED – SUPPORT SYSTEMS, SKILLS, ETC.?

4. WHAT DO YOU CHOOSE TO DO DIFFERENTLY?

5. **WHAT DID YOU LEARN? ANY SURPRISES? WHAT ARE YOUR NEXT STEPS ON THE WAY OF WISDOM?**

After you have responded to these final questions, jot down the date at the end of your responses. Then, when you revisit these questions in the integration process, you will be able to acknowledge your progress. You may later add responses to these questions as you continue to reflect on realizing your vision.

Mountain 10 Quadrant Reflections

LETTING GO   VISION

AWARENESS   REALIZATION

Chapter 5:
MOUNTAIN 10. CHANGE CYCLE

This chapter is for the seasoned climber, one who has made the Mountain 10 journey several times and is acquainted with the quadrants and turns of the LABgraphic. Mountain 10 Change Cycle is an adaptation of the Mountain 10 technology that highlights the change process through the use of four colors: yellow, red, blue and green. This experience requires familiarity with the LAB-graphic path and process. In the Mountain 10 Change Cycle process, each quadrant is identified with a color. At each waypoint, climbers change colors to symbolize the particular terrain through which they are climbing. Switching colors as you journey through the terrains can deepen the questions and insights related to the four quadrants.

You will follow the same path, attending to the same terrains, but you will change colors at each waypoint. The alternating colors highlight how the terrains flow into each other and how the change process is a dialogical conversation among the dimensions of *Awareness, Letting Go, Vision,* and *Realization*. Before you begin Mountain 10 Change Cycle, spend a few minutes journaling with the questions provided on pages 62-63 about your everyday experiences with the four colors of yellow, red, blue and green. You may enter the LAB-graphic path with an intention that you have used before or with a different question or critical concern. Often, Mountain 10 Change Cycle will bring new insights and images to your mind and heart as you explore the terrains with a deep awareness of their inter-relationships.

Using the four colors of the terrains: *Awareness (yellow), Letting Go (red), Vision (blue)* and *Realization (green)*, we can literally see the interplay in the reflective process that leads to change. Applying the colors of the terrains makes us more aware of the internal process of insight that spirals deeper as we move through the quadrants of the LABgraphic. The frequencies and wavelengths of the colors create a visual dance that influences us on both the physical and emotional level. The iterative movement through the terrains creates a rhythmic dance as we switch colors at each waypoint. The cyclical process of change appears in the flow of color through the quadrants. In Mountain 10 Change Cycle, the four colors help us recognize our shifts in consciousness as we travel back and forth through the terrains of interiority.

These four colors have meanings and associations for each one of us. What do you associate with the color yellow? Sunshine, mustard, daffodils, jaundice? What does red symbolize for you? Passion, anger, spirit, destruction? When you think of blue do you recall a perfect summer sky or the ominous clouds of an oncoming storm? When you reflect on your experience with green, do you think of cool, dewy grass, toxic ooze, or a perfect leaf tapping at your window? Take several minutes to journal about your experience of these four colors--yellow, red, blue and green--using the following questions.

Journaling Questions on Colors

List 3 things, experiences, memories, etc. associated with the color yellow. As you think of each of these responses, what feelings arise in you?

List 3 things, experiences, memories, etc. associated with the color red. As you think of each of these responses, what feelings arise in you?

List 3 things, experiences, memories, etc. associated with the color blue. As you think of each of these responses, what feelings arise in you?

List 3 things, experiences, memories, etc. associated with the color green. As you think of each of these responses, what feelings arise you?

Now you are ready to embark on Mountain 10 Change Cycle with a greater awareness of your own experiences and feelings with color and a deeper sensitivity to the way colors pull images, memories and insights out of us. As with the Mountain 10 climb, we will lead you through the process step by step

Prayer Flags at Mount Everest. Colorful Buddhist prayer flags fly in the crisp mountain wind with the iconic summit of Mount Everest in the background. The four colors of Mountain 10 Change Cycle deepen our attention to the dimensions of the change process.

The Power of Intention

As with Mountain 10, the outcome of this experience is highly dependent upon your intention or purpose. When your intention is clear, you will discover the way to achieve it. Wisdom will come to you if you intend to receive it, if you are clear about the question, issue or challenge you are facing. The most important question is What do you really want? What's in your heart? There are many distractions that call for our energy and commitment. Our stories may contain examples of seeking things that did not bring us joy. Now is the time to focus on what matters. What do you really want? Only you can answer that question. Intention is the energy behind the manifestation of your vision.

As you are about to begin your journey, take this time to quiet yourself and reflect; then write down your intention.

What do you really want?

Tools

Ropes, anchors, stoppers and cams are NOT the tools you will need for this climb. You will need silence—a minimum of one uninterrupted hour of precious time. You will need intention, crystal clear intention, about what you really want. You will need focus, attention to how you are feeling and awareness of what you are thinking on the way. There will be many distractions but with focus you will return again and again to your clear intention and what you are learning from yourself. You will need openness—the willingness to let the new into your consciousness, to not judge a new thought or feeling or intuition harshly, and to see the profound wisdom at the core of who you are. **Finally, you will need four crayons: yellow, red, blue and green.** Follow the directions carefully.

DIRECTIONS FOR THE JOURNEY:

- Take several breaths to settle yourself for the task at hand. Pay attention to your feeling, thinking, seeing and hearing (inner and outer voice). Bring your intention clearly to your mind and heart. Hold close the intention you have written to the question "What do you really, really want?"

- Observe the LABgraphic Change Cycle on page 67, looking carefully at the four quadrants marked by name and color: YELLOW/ Awareness, RED/ Letting Go, BLUE/ Vision and GREEN/ Realization. As you come to each waypoint, change your crayon color to correspond with the quadrant color you are in. Reflect on the quadrant you are in and its implication for your intention. Stay focused on your journey as you change color and direction, coloring the path and going at your own pace.

- Begin: Let go of your expectations. Press the tip of your forefinger on the waypoint at the entrance to the LABgraphic Change Cycle. Feel your pulse. Notice where you are and remember who you are. Recall your intention. Take one deep breath. Using the YELLOW crayon, enter the path.

- You have crossed the threshold into your inner adventure. Fully color in the path YELLOW as you go until you reach the first waypoint, which is in the LETTING GO quadrant. Color the waypoint RED. You may want to write down what you are thinking or feeling about your INTENTION in this LETTING GO quadrant or terrain. A sheet of paper with the four quadrants (Quadrant Reflections, page 75) is provided for you if you wish to jot down thoughts and feelings as you move through the terrains of the LABgraphic Change Cycle.

- Color in the path RED until you reach the second waypoint. Color the waypoint YELLOW. You may want to write down what you are thinking or feeling about your INTENTION in this AWARENESS quadrant.

- Color in the path YELLOW until you reach the third waypoint. Color the waypoint RED. Reflect on the terrain of LETTING GO and its implications for your intention.

- Color in the path RED until you reach the fourth waypoint. Color the waypoint BLUE. Reflect on the terrain of VISION and its implications for your intention.

- Color in the path BLUE until you reach the fifth waypoint. Color the waypoint GREEN. Reflect on the terrain of REALIZATION and its implications for your intention.
- Color in the path GREEN until you reach the sixth waypoint. Color the waypoint BLUE. Reflect on the terrain of VISION and its implications for your intention.

- Color in the path BLUE until you reach the seventh waypoint. Color the waypoint RED. Reflect on the terrain of LETTING GO and its implications for your intention.

- Color in the path RED until you reach the eighth waypoint. Color the waypoint YELLOW. Reflect on the terrain of AWARENESS and its implications for your intention.

- Color in the path YELLOW until you reach the ninth waypoint. Color the waypoint RED. Reflect on the terrain of LETTING GO and its implications for your intention.

- Color in the path RED until you reach waypoint 10, Mountain 10, which is colored red. At this point, STOP. Put the crayons aside and look at your journey. Reflect on the questions on page 68 (Questions at Mountain 10 Waypoint: Writing Your Own Story), jotting down your answers if you wish.

MOUNTAIN 10 . LABgraphic
Change Cycle

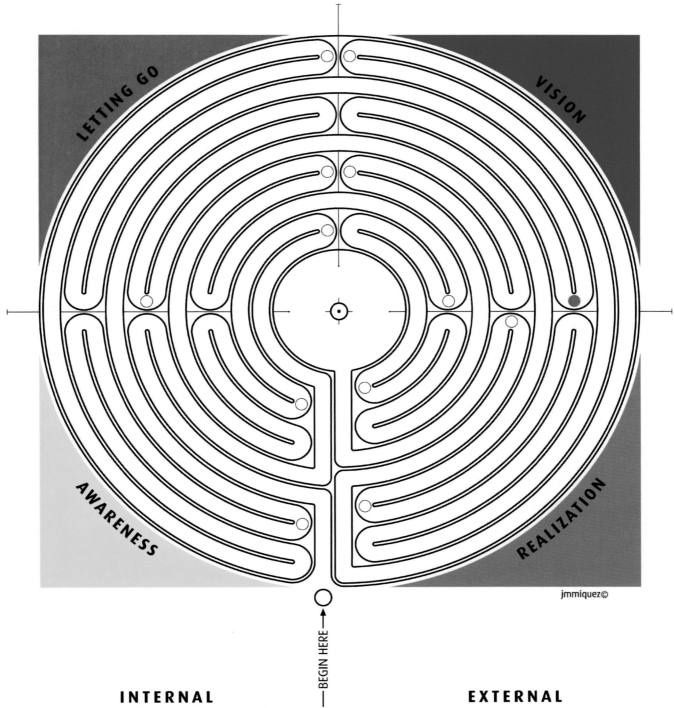

LETTING GO

VISION

AWARENESS

REALIZATION

BEGIN HERE

INTERNAL

EXTERNAL

jmmiquez©

Questions at Mountain 10 Waypoint: Writing Your Own Story

Look at the LABgraphic Change Cycle from different points of view. With a sense of play and exploration, look at your climb from multiple perspectives, turning the book, changing your angle of view. Notice how far you've come. Pay attention to what is colored in and what is yet to come. What did you see or notice during your climb so far?

What were you feeling during your climb? What are you feeling now?

What were you thinking during your climb? What are you thinking now?

What happened? Did you experience anything unexpected?

What insights do you have now?

- After you have considered the Questions at Mountain 10 Waypoint, use the BLUE crayon to color in the rest of the way to the summit, again being aware of the quadrants through which you are moving. If you wish, jot down any thoughts and feelings as they occur in this final part of the climb to the summit.

- Make your way to the CENTER of the LABgraphic Change Cycle, to the summit, the higher ground from which you can see the whole. Place your forefinger on the center, feel your pulse, notice where you are and who you are. Take three deep breaths. Rest here. Take whatever time you need before you begin your return. Be fully present in your body, mind and spirit.

- THE RETURN: Ultimately Mountain 10 Change Cycle is about the return—returning home with the gifts and insights of the journey. Now with your finger, trace your way through the LABgraphic Change Cycle, down the mountain, remembering your journey, being aware of the quadrants which you are passing through again. Can you take the wisdom you have touched and bring it back home? What is required for you to make your new story come alive? Going down the mountain may be more difficult than the climb up. Be careful with each step. Hold on to your intention as you descend the mountain. Remember, it is about the return.

- When you arrive at the entrance to the pathway, stop. Be fully present, take three deep breaths and be conscious about taking your first step back into your everyday reality. The climb is over AND it is just beginning. Be grateful for the journey, appreciate your own story. Revisit the intention you wrote down on page 65. What do you really want?

- Take a few minutes to answer the Mountain 10 Change Cycle Final Reflection Questions on pages 70-74. Jot down the date you complete each answer so you can keep track of your different responses as you continue to reflect on these questions through the integration process.

Mountain 10 Change Cycle Final Reflection Questions

1. WHAT NO LONGER BRINGS YOU JOY OR TAKES YOU AWAY FROM YOUR SOURCE? WHAT DO YOU CHOOSE TO LET GO?

2. **WHAT BRINGS YOU JOY AND IS IN ALIGNMENT WITH YOUR SOURCE? WHAT DO YOU CHOOSE TO KEEP?**

3. WHAT DO YOU CHOOSE TO ADD TO KEEP YOUR SOURCE FUELED – SUPPORT SYSTEMS, SKILLS, ETC.?

4. WHAT DO YOU CHOOSE TO DO DIFFERENTLY?

5. **WHAT DID YOU LEARN? ANY SURPRISES? WHAT ARE YOUR NEXT STEPS ON THE WAY OF WISDOM?**

After you have responded to these final questions, jot down the date at the end of your responses. Then, when you revisit these questions in the integration process, you will be able to acknowledge your progress. You may later add responses to these questions as you continue to reflect on realizing your vision.

Mountain 10 Change Cycle Quadrant Reflections

LETTING GO (Red)   VISION (Blue)

AWARENESS (Yellow)   REALIZATION (Green)

Chapter 6:
CONTINUING THE JOURNEY

Dreaming, visioning and planning are only preparatory steps in the challenging journey of living your passion and values. Mountain 10 provides a safe and generative space for listening to the heart's urge, the soul's true song. However, the real work is in the return, integrating the insights of the Mountain 10 climb into the everyday commitments and concerns of your life. To live in tune with what you really want, your deepest longings, the values that are at the core of who you are, requires intentional focus and sustained effort. Some plod with persistent small steps toward their new vision. Others take bold leaps of deep change that often evoke resistance and confusion from others.

Whether your personality steps or leaps through the change process, you will begin to experience the sweet music of living in harmony with your core, rather than the discord of having aspects of your life out of tune with what you really want. When you begin to realize your vision, even if there is internal and external resistance, you will experience an inner sense of congruence. Your life will begin to feel whole and connected, rather than scattered and piecemeal. You will have a sense of integrity and alignment about who you are and what you do. Through the process of integration, what you are yearning for on the inside and what you are doing on the outside will mesh more often. Closing the gap between vision and realization requires continuing work, step by step, action by action. Patience and persistence are the necessary virtues for this arduous work.

In many religious and cultural traditions there is the belief that each of us is born for a particular purpose or with specific gifts and contributions to make to the world. When we take our unique place in our community and live out our singular calling, we have a deep sense of joy and satisfaction, even though life may hold difficulty and pain. In *Wisdom of the Heart*, Alan Cohen writes that in a particular African tribe when a woman becomes pregnant she goes deep into the forest to listen to the song of the child growing within her because each person has a particular music and vibration. When the child comes into the world, the community sings the child's song in welcome. As the child goes through the stages of life in the community, the people gather and sing the person's song to remind the individual of the unique music that only this person can bring into the world.[1]

> When we reach a "critical mass" of integration, we experience spontaneous combustion—an explosion of inner synergy that ignites the fire within and gives vision, passion, and a spirit of adventure to life.
>
> **Stephen Covey**

Living with Integrity

The Mountain 10 journey reminds us of the song that belongs to us, the song of our true purpose and identity. Integrating the wisdom from our Mountain 10 climb means learning to sing that song proudly and confidently on the mountain tops and in the valleys of our lives. When we live with integrity and sing our unique song, there is harmony between the inner and outer person. Parker Palmer calls this joining soul and role. He says,

> If our roles were more deeply informed by the truth that is in our souls, the general level of sanity and safety would rise dramatically. A teacher who shares his or her identity with students is more effective than one who lobs factoids at them from behind a wall. A supervisor who leads from personal authenticity gets better work out of people than one who leads from a script. A doctor who invests selfhood in his or her practice is a better healer than one who treats patients at arm's length.[2]

When we join soul and role, act with integrity, and live from our boldest vision, we experience a sense of harmony that flows into our relationships and our work. We tend to experience greater vitality and satisfaction. When our acts are consistent with our core values, those who engage with us in our personal and professional lives often recognize that we are acting with authenticity and integrity. When we live from the soul outward, we engender trust and collaboration. Slowly, living our vision begins to bear fruit in right relationships and good work.

In the following pages, we suggest several strategies that may be helpful in this process of integration. Just as with the Mountain 10 climb, individuals must trust their own rhythm and timing in bringing their vision to full realization. There isn't a right pace or a minimum or maximum time frame for completing the integration process. However, it is very important to identify the concrete steps toward realization. If you do not set goals, deadlines and measurements, you will never know if you are making headway. When you make your goals specific with concrete actions, you are able to measure your progress. As with the Mountain 10 journey, this isn't a linear process. Rather, you return again and again to consider your vision and how to fully realize it. The path will continue to reveal itself if you are open and willing to explore.

We recommend that you regularly "work the questions." Review your responses to the final questions of Mountain 10 at least once a month. Take a few minutes to center yourself by breathing deeply. Bring your attention to one question. Be fully present to the question and your previous response. Ask yourself what you are continuing to learn about this question. Jot down any new insights that have occurred to you about what you really want. Remember to date your new responses. As you return to the questions repeatedly, you will bring new perspectives and viewpoints to your reflection. There is a spiral movement to this process. Each time you consider the questions, the process deepens and expands.

Another activity that many have found helpful is to talk with a trusted friend or colleague about your Mountain 10 climb. If possible, engage a friend, spouse or small group of colleagues to experience Mountain 10 and share reflections soon after. We suggest three basic ground rules for this sharing. First, agree with one another that there will be no fixing, counseling or advice giving. Simply be present and listen. Second, it is very important to commit to confidentiality together so that your conversation can be open and free of the fear that it might be shared with others. Third, be conscious of the time and giving each person the time they need.

GROUND RULES FOR SHARING

1. Be fully present and listen.
2. Avoid fixing, counseling or giving advice.
3. Commit to confidentiality.
4. Give each person the time they need.

The focus of the conversation is to help persons continue to access their deepest wisdom, to find their own answers and listen to the voice within. Give each person the time they need to speak, to share as much as they wish about the experience, how they answered some of the key questions or what feelings were raised during the journey. The other person or persons will listen deeply to the information that is being shared, as well as to the feelings and values that are being communicated. You might consider a brief time of silence after the individual has shared. Then, the listener or listeners ask open-ended questions that might help the individual who is sharing to go more deeply into their own internal wisdom. Each question is presented with space for a reply but no expectation. Use open-ended questions, not focused on specific information. Here are some examples of open-ended questions: What has your past experience taught you about this question or issue? What is your gut telling you about this? If you could look at this issue from the perspective of five years in the future, what might you see? What else? What did you think of saying but didn't say and why? Be careful of questions that are actually camouflaged advice, such as "Do you think you need professional help with this issue?" To ask a question that will potentially open the speaker to another dimension of their own inner wisdom is an exceptional art. The key is to focus on the well-being of the speaker and let go of any of your own assumptions and experiences. The speaker can answer the questions or simply consider them in silence. After each person has had the opportunity to speak and to listen, close the sharing with simple expressions of gratitude.

...then I was standing on the highest mountain of them all, and round about beneath me was the whole hoop of the world...

Black Elk

Deepen Your Insights Through Sharing

For centuries the Quakers have used this kind of process for personal and communal discernment. In his ground-breaking work with teachers and leaders, Parker Palmer has developed the basic Quaker practice into a process that creates a powerful circle of trust in which the soul is encouraged to speak. According to Palmer, "a circle of trust holds us in a space where we can make our own discernments, in our own way and time, in the encouraging and challenging presence of other people."[3] The attentive listening of others and their helpful questions can deepen our insights on our journey. We are challenged to consider our new learning and to listen to the voice of wisdom within. Also, having someone else on the journey makes it less daunting. We are not alone. At the same time, the witness of another holds us accountable. We are more apt to follow through on our commitments when someone else knows that we have made them.

To live our vision requires that we do things differently, change old habits, develop new virtues. As with any change process, practice is the key ingredient to bringing about the desired outcome. Although different studies suggest different time frames, integrating even a minor change requires at least seven days and major changes may require twenty-one days or three months or a year. Like our computers, we have developed a default setting when it comes to many of the repetitive experiences in our lives. We unconsciously react with our habitual behavior. When we take the time to consciously and regularly reflect on our actions and decisions, we can catch ourselves before we simply follow our default setting. We can learn to recognize circumstances and comments that "push our buttons." We can notice when we are about to launch into our old mode of behavior. In these situations, it is best to pause, breathe deeply, reflect on our vision and make a choice that is consistent with our best possibilities. This simple process is based on the four-step approach to reducing stress found in *The Wellness Book*: stop, breathe, reflect, choose.[4] Maintaining physical, psychological or spiritual health requires living with greater awareness in the present moment so that we can make wise choices that embody our vision.

Even when we are deeply committed to integrating our vision and realizing our dreams, we can get off track. We make self-defeating choices. When we do, it is critical that we cultivate an attitude of self-forgiveness. We can be gentle with ourselves. This doesn't mean that we rationalize and make excuses for actions that are inconsistent with our highest purpose. Rather, we recognize our shortcomings and imperfections. We can also recognize that every poor choice is an opportunity to learn more about ourselves and the difficult situations we encounter. Rather than focusing on perfection, it is important to make consistent progress toward the full realization of our vision. The mountain climber knows that when the way gets steep, it is best to keep putting one foot in front of the other. Be present to the danger and the beauty of the climb. Pause and reflect often. Keep going. Even small steps are important gains in the difficult work of realizing our deepest longings.

Obstacles are those frightful things you see when you take your eyes off your goal.

Henry Ford

Courage doesn't always roar. Sometimes courage is the little voice at the end of the day that says I'll try again tomorrow.

Mary Anne Radmacher

80

Labyrinth Gathering Event, Omega Center, Rhinebeck, New York. Modern labyrinths have been used throughout the United States and Europe and around the world at retreat centers, hospitals, community education sites, churches, and many other places. This photo shows a unique neon labyrinth created on canvas.

Skills for Integration

There are two kinds of skills that are particularly important in the process of integration—imaginal skills and systems skills. As with other skills, we develop them through practice, by doing them repeatedly and consistently. Imaginal skills include all of the ways we see, consider and open ourselves to the possible. We give form and urgency to our dreams through our imaginations. When we consider alternatives and attempt to expand our view of what is viable in a situation, we are practicing imaginal skills. When we set aside our assumptions to permit a different way of seeing and thinking, we are flexing the muscles of our imaginations. When we ask our colleagues to approach a challenge from a different angle or take time to enlarge the possible solutions, we are growing our imaginal skills. Being open to the imagination is not easy. There is often significant pressure to do things the way we've always done them, to practice convergent thinking rather than divergent thinking. Divergent thinking requires stepping into a place of ambiguity and discomfort. It involves admitting the limits of our knowledge and our abilities of prediction. It also requires a deep sense of trust both internally and externally with our colleagues, friends and family. When we envision the ideal, we often are labeled unrealistic. Often the term "dreamer" is used pejoratively. "Fantasy" carries with it a sense of impracticality. Yet, integrating our vision calls us to be dreamers and idealists. When we can imagine the possible, give it shape, consider its outcomes, and believe in its promises, we have the imaginative muscle to realize our dreams.

SKILLS FOR INTEGRATION

Imaginal Skills:
1. Think of alternatives.
2. Set aside assumptions.
3. Approach from a different angle.
4. Imagine the possible.

Systems Skills:
1. See the parts and the whole.
2. Identify patterns and structures.
3. Notice relationships.
4. Negotiate complexity.

Systems skills identify another set of key abilities important for the integration process. The systems of education, civic engagement, governmental agencies, cultural expectations, religious organizations, family structures and so many others have a very significant influence on our lives. We may feel hemmed in by the various systems that impact our lives minute to minute. Systems skills include a deep awareness of how the various systems of our society work and how the parts affect the whole. Such skills involve learning how to negotiate the complexities of institutions, policies and multiple expectations. Systems skills help us manage our relationships, time, money and priorities. How do I manage my time and meet the needs of my family if I go back to school? How do I manage my money if I take the lower paying job that allows for more vacation and free time? How do I manage my priorities and continue to nurture the relationships of my blended family if I become the board chair of an important non-profit agency in my community? Some people feel stuck in a job because they can't afford to leave it. They have a mortgage to pay and kids to feed and interior expectations about economic and social achievement. Only when we recognize the complex web of systems that play out in our lives can we begin to make changes. Only when we see the ways in which the systems of our lives are inter-related can we determine what steps move us effectively toward the realization of our boldest visions.

The integration process often involves expanding the circle of those who are attentive to their interior wisdom. When we have colleagues, friends and family who have made the Mountain 10 climb, there is often a synergistic effect. When others who are connected to us are taking the path of inner wisdom seriously, we have powerful conversations about the change process. There is a deeper sense of respect for each person as they follow the call that they are hearing within. Often,

Systems thinking is a discipline for seeing wholes. It is a framework for seeing interrelationships rather than things, for seeing patterns of change rather than static "snapshots."

Peter Senge

there is greater openness to exploring reflective processes together, such as journaling or meditation. What is difficult to do alone is more easily accomplished with mutual support and concern.

As you consider ways to expand the circle of those who are Mountain 10 climbers, consider using Mountain 10 as part of a team development process. Mountain 10 helps people focus on what they really want for themselves and the team. When people share their deep wisdom, new levels of collaboration and trust often result. Mountain 10 can also be very effective as part of a personal or organizational decision-making process. Each person enters the LABgraphic with their decision and allows the quadrants of awareness, letting go, vision and realization to deepen their consideration of their choice. Some organizations and groups have used Mountain 10 as a prelude to a planning process. People have remarked how quickly the planning process goes when they have considered beforehand what they really want. Each person, then, comes to the process with greater focus and a deeper awareness of what their major goals might require.

Mountain 10 can be used in many contexts. Clients for counseling have an opportunity to focus their attention on what may be most meaningful for their personal development. Mediators may use Mountain 10 as a way to help participants clarify what they really want out of the process. Mountain 10 can be helpful in relationships to determine priorities for continuing growth. It can help families identify key issues for dialogue. Students can use it to consider their career path. It gives job seekers a process for considering what they really seek in employment. It can help persons who are entering a spiritual direction relationship to identify particular areas for exploration. Through the Mountain 10 climb, new awareness, insight and vision emerges for individuals and groups.

The Mountain 10 climb is never complete. Way leads onto way. New paths open before us as we consider the wisest possibilities for our lives. As we enter into different seasons of our family life, our careers, and our personal lives, we continue to seek what we really want. We continue to deepen our awareness, become freer in our letting go, dream more boldly and realize more fully our most profound possibilities for a joyful and meaningful life. Wisdom is within. It will teach us the way.

NOTE: The process of integration and the development of imaginal and systems skills requires practice and more practice. The necessary disciplines are often made easier if we have partners, mentors and coaches to practice with us and share their experience. As you continue the integration process, you may find it helpful to join the virtual Mountain 10 community at www.MountainTen.com. Stories of fellow climbers often inspire us when the way gets difficult. You can connect with others who have had similar experiences and share similar values. We also provide retreats, workshops and virtual learning communities that may be helpful on the path of integration. For many, personal coaching is a key strategy

Never confuse a clear view of the future with a short distance.

Paul Saffo

To finish the moment, to find the journey's end in every step of the road, to live the greatest number of good hours is wisdom.

Ralph Waldo Emerson

for sustaining momentum in the change process. A listing of personal coaches who are trained in the Mountain 10 process is provided on the website. You will also find links to other organizations that are doing work consistent with our vision of paying attention to the deep wisdom within. As we explore new technologies for accessing our rich sources of inner wisdom, we make these available at www. MountainTen.com.

JOURNALING QUESTIONS

How can I enlarge the circle of those who are paying attention to their own inner wisdom?

How can I practice the skills of imagination?

What systems are having the greatest impact in my life? How am I being called to respond?

What one step that I can take within the next month would move me most clearly toward the fulfillment of my vision?

Labyrinth 6/95

Enter it I go, mind wondering, soon to see. The path wanders and winds like the freedom given to searching thoughts, ideas, solutions.

Here , there, where?

Diverge we explore, contained within each step controlling convergence keeps us on the path.

Where do we go?
Where are we going?
Where is our goal?

Towards it? Away? Our mind tries to pull away, to seek the un-seeable future.

More steps, turns, and winding travel and out of the maze springs the map of life compassed by our trust to follow our inner selves, our inner know. In. Out. Turn, back, forth we journey toward our desired next step...

Mike Donahue
Deceased master climber, guide, and founder of Colorado Mountain School

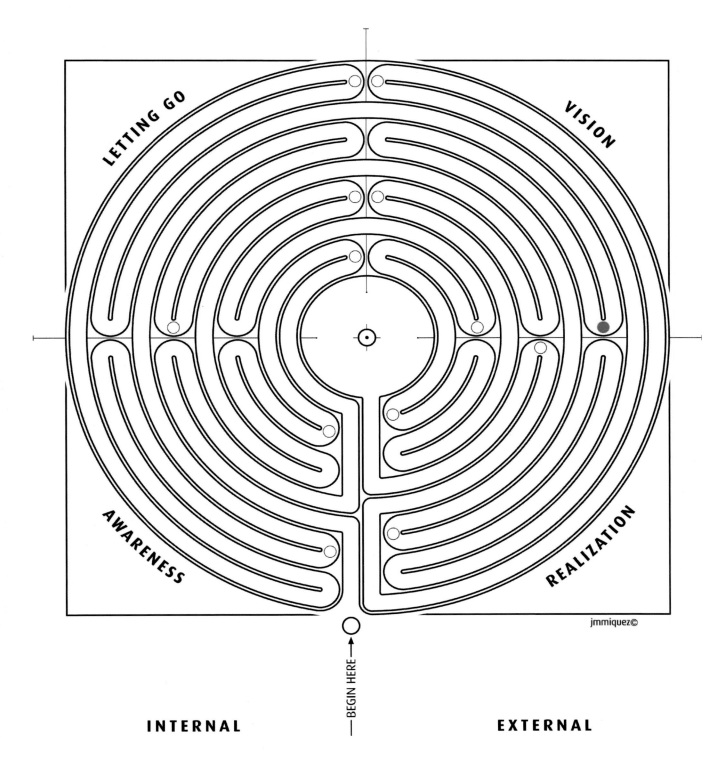

jmmiquez©

BEGIN HERE

INTERNAL

EXTERNAL

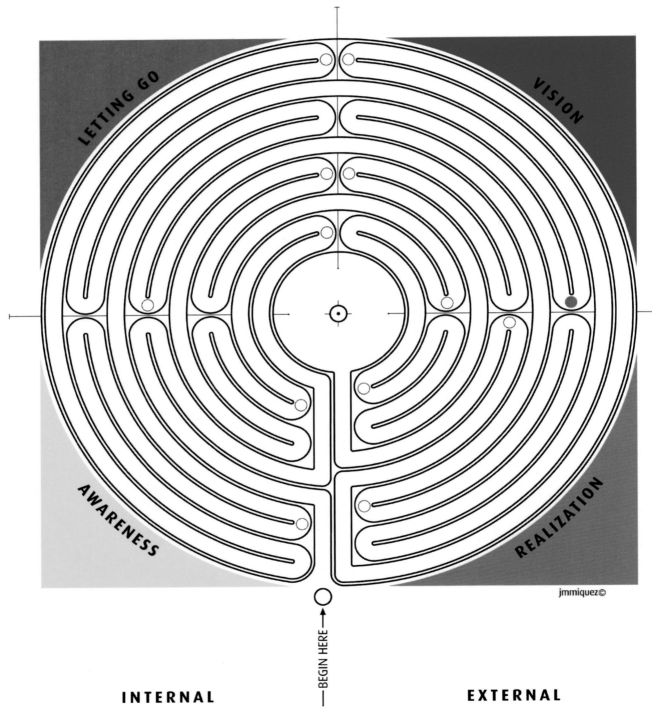

jmmiquez©

INTERNAL   **EXTERNAL**

BEGIN HERE

NOTES

Chapter One: Wisdom Within

1. Cecilia Chan, Petula Sik Ying Ho and Esther Chow, "A Body-Mind-Spirit Model in Health: An Eastern Approach," *Social Work in Healthcare* 34 (2001): 261-2.
2. Taken from the website of the 100 People Foundation, http://www.100people.org/statistics_100stats.php?section=statistics accessed on August 1, 2012
3. Gary J. Boelhower, "Sanctuary" in *Marrow, Muscle, Flight* (Duluth: Wildwood River Press, 2011), 45.
4. Benjamin Hoff , *The Tao of Pooh* (New York: Penguin, 1994), 153.
5. Parker J. Palmer, *Let Your Life Speak: Listening for the Voice of Vocation* (San Francisco: Jossey-Bass, 2000), 79.
6. Rainer Maria Rilke, *Letters to a Young Poet*, trans. M. D. Herter (New York: Norton, 1993), p. 35.
7. Matthew Lipman, *Elfie* (Upper Montclair, New Jersey: Institute for the Advancement of Philosophy for Children, 1988), 157.
8. Ibid., 164, 183.
9. Margaret Wheatley, keynote address at "Servant Leadership and Community Leadership in the 21st Century," June 10-13, 1999, Indianapolis, Indiana.
10. Warren G. Bennis, *On Becoming a Leader* (Cambridge, Massachusetts: Perseus Books, 1989), 40.
11. There are many translations of these final words of the Buddha. See: http://www.artofdharma.org/archives/be-a-light-unto-yourself.html or http://www.sacred-texts.com/bud/btg/btg94.htm or http://www.shambhalasun.com/index.php?option=content&task=view&id=1644
12. quote from Carl G. Jung, see http://thinkexist.com/quotation/your_vision_will_become_clear_only_when_you_look/12978.html
13. Candace Pert, *Your Body Is Your Subconscious Mind*, 3 CD Set Audio Recording (Boulder, CO: Sounds True, 2005).

Chapter Two: Wisdom Technologies Ancient and New

1. Carl G. Jung et al., *Man and His Symbols* (New York: Dell Publishing, 1968).
2. Richard Bach, *Jonathan Livingston Seagull* (New York: Scribner, 2006). First published in 1970.
3. L. Frank Baum, *The Wonderful Wizard of Oz* (New York: Simon and Brown, 2012). First published in 1900.
4. Erik H. Erikson, *Childhood and Society* (New York: W. W. Norton and Company, 1993). First published in 1950.
5. T.S. Eliot, *Four Quartets* (New York: Harcourt, Brace and Company, 1943), 39.
6. Parker J. Palmer, *Let Your Life Speak: Listening for the Voice of Vocation* (San Francisco: Jossey-Bass, 2000), 96.
7. Edward Hirsch, "My Pace Provokes My Thoughts," *The American Poetry Review*, 40, 2 (2011): 5.
8. Ibid, 10.
9. Joseph Campbell, *Hero with a Thousand Faces* (Princeton, New Jersey: Princeton University Press, 1968).
10. quoted from Gillian Corcoran, "Healing the Planet One Step at a Time" from http://www.ambassadors4peace.org/Newsletters/Stories/Mar06/labyrinths.htm
11. see http://crossroads.spps.org/Peace_Labyrinth.html

Chapter Three: Preparing for Mountain 10

1. Gary J. Boelhower, "Sanctuary" in *Marrow, Muscle, Flight* (Duluth: Wildwood River Press, 2011), 45.

Chapter Six: Continuing the Journey

1. Adam Cohen, *Wisdom of the Heart: Inspiration for a Life Worth Living* (Carlsbad, California: Hay House, 2002), 10.
2. Parker J. Palmer, *A Hidden Wholeness: The Journey Toward an Undivided Life* (San Francisco: Jossey-Bass, 2004), 17.
3. Ibid., 27.
4. Herbert Benson and Eileen M. Stuart, *The Wellness Book: The Comprehensive Guide to Maintaining Health and Treating Stress-Related Illness* (New York: Scribner, 1992, 2010), 184.

WORKS CITED

Bach, Richard. *Jonathan Livingston Seagull.* New York: Scribner, 2006.

Baum, L. Frank. *The Wonderful Wizard of Oz.* New York: Simon and Brown, 2012.

Bennis, Warren G. *On Becoming a Leader.* Cambridge, Massachusetts: Perseus Books, 1989.

Benson, Herbert and Stuart, Eileen M. *The Wellness Book: The Comprehensive Guide to Maintaining Health and Treating Stress-Related Illness.* New York: Scribner, 1992, 2010.

Boelhower, Gary J. *Marrow, Muscle, Flight.* Duluth, Minnesota: Wildwood River Press, 2011.

Campbell, Joseph. *Hero with a Thousand Faces.* Princeton, New Jersey: Princeton University Press, 1968.

Chan, Cecilia, Petula Sik Ying Ho and Esther Chow. "A Body-Mind-Spirit Model in Health: An Eastern Approach." *Social Work in Healthcare* 34 (2001): 261-82.

Cohen, Adam. *Wisdom of the Heart: Inspiration for a Life Worth Living.* Carlsbad, California: Hay House, 2002.

Eliot, T.S. *Four Quartets.* New York: Harcourt, Brace and Company, 1943.

Erikson, Erik H. *Childhood and Society.* New York: W. W. Norton and Company, 1993.

Hirsch, Edward. "My Pace Provokes My Thoughts," *The American Poetry Review,* 40, 2 2011

Hoff, Benjamin. *The Tao of Pooh.* New York: Penguin, 1994.

Jung, Carl G. *Man and His Symbols.* New York: Dell Publishing, 1964.

Lipman, Matthew. *Elfie.* Upper Montclair, New Jersey: Institute for the Advancement of Philosophy for Children, 1988.

Palmer, Parker J. *A Hidden Wholeness: The Journey Toward an Undivided Life.* San Francisco: Jossey-Bass, 2004.

_____. *Let Your Life Speak: Listening for the Voice of Vocation.* San Francisco: Jossey-Bass, 2000.

Pert, Candace. *Your Body Is Your Subconscious Mind.* 3 CD Set Audio Recording, Boulder, Colorado: Sounds True, 2005.

Rilke, Rainer Maria. *Letters to a Young Poet.* trans. M. D. Herter, New York: Norton, 1993.

RECOMMENDED READING

Abbott, Edwin A. *Flatland: A Romance of Many Dimensions*. New York: Dover, 1992.

Arrien, Angeles. *The Four Fold Way: Walking the Paths of the Warrior, Teacher, Healer, and Visionary*. New York: HarperOne. 1993.

Artress, Lauren. *Walking a Sacred Path: Rediscovering the Labyrinth as a Spiritual Practice*. New York: Riverhead Books, 1995.

Atwater, P. M. H. *Future Memory*. Charlottesville, Virginia: Hampton Roads Publishing Company, 1999.

Beck, Don Edward and Cowan, Christopher. *Spiral Dynamics: Mastering Values, Leadership and Change*. Maiden, Massachusetts: Wiley-Blackwell, 2005.

Braden, Gregg. *The God Code: The Secret of Our Past, The Promise of Our Future*. Carlsbad, California: Hay House, 2005.

Bridges, William. *Transitions: Making Sense of Life's Changes*. New York: De Capo Press, 2004.

Campbell, Joseph with Bill Moyers. *The Power of Myth*. New York: Anchor Doubleday, 1988.

Cooperrider, David and Diana Whitney. *Appreciative Inquiry: A Positive Revolution in Change*. San Francisco: Berrett-Koehler, 2005.

Daumal, René. *Mount Analogue*. trans. by Carol Cosman. New York: Overlook Press, Peter Mayer Publishers, 2010.

De Jongh, Paul. *Our Common Journey: A Pioneering Approach to Cooperative Environmental Management*. London: Zed Books Ltd, 1999.

Fritz, Robert. *The Path of Least Resistance*. New York: Fawcett Books, 1984.

Goleman, Daniel. *Emotional Intelligence: Tenth Anniversary Edition*. New York: Bantam, 2006.

Heim, Michael. *The Metaphysics of Virtual Reality*. New York: Oxford University Press, 1994.

Isaacs, William. *Dialogue and the Art of Thinking Together*. New York: Random House, 1999.

Mendoza, Ramon. *The Acentric Labyrinth: Giordano Bruno's Prelude to Contemporary Cosmology*, Rockport, Massachusetts, 1995.

Myss, Caroline. *Anatomy of the Spirit: The Seven Stages of Power and Healing*. New York: Three Rivers Press, 1996.

Neal, Judi. *Edgewalkers: People and Organizations that Take Risks, Build Bridges, and Break New Ground*. Westport, CT: Praeger, 2006.

Newberg, Andrew, D'Aquili, Eugene and Rause, Vince. *Why God Won't Go Away: Brain Science and the Biology of Belief.* New York: Ballantine, 2001.

Plotkin, Bill. *Soulcraft: Crossing into the Mysteries of Nature and Psyche.* Novato, CA: New World Library, 2003.

Richardson, Peter Tufts. *Four Spiritualities: Expressions of Self, Expressions of Spirit: A Psychology of Contemporary Spiritual Choice.* Palo Alto, California: Davies-Black Publishing, 1996.

Rockwell, Irini. *The Five Wisdom Energies: A Buddhist Way of Understanding Personalities, Emotions and Relationships.* Boston: Shambhala, 2002.

Ruiz, Don Miquel. *The Four Agreements: A Practical Guide to Personal Freedom..* San Rafael, California: Amber-Allen Publishing, 1997.

Senge, Peter M., Art Kleiner, Richard Ross, Bryan Smith, and Charlotte Roberts. *The Fifth Discipline Fieldbook.* New York: Doubleday, 1994

Smith, Rolf. *The Seven Levels of Change: Different Thinking for Different Results.* Wyomissing, Pennsylvania: Tapestry Press, 2007.

Tolle, Eckhart. *Awakening to Your Life's Purpose.* New York: Penquin, 2006.

ABOUT THE AUTHORS

Gary Boelhower, Ph.D.

 Gary teaches ethics, spirituality, and leadership at The College of St. Scholastica in Duluth, Minnesota. He has served in leadership capacities in higher education, including Chair of Humanities, Dean of Life-Long Learning, Dean of Graduate Studies and Vice President for Academic Affairs. He co-founded and was first Director of the Center for Spirituality and Leadership at Marian University in Fond du Lac, Wisconsin. He writes, consults, coaches and speaks on dialogue, authentic leadership, values and vision, wise decision-making, professional ethics and the respectful workplace. His recent collection of poetry *Marrow, Muscle, Flight* won the Midwest Book Award in 2011. His book *Choose Wisely: Practical Insights from Spiritual Traditions* was published by Paulist Press in 2013.

Joe Miguez, B.A.

Joe has been involved with the concept, symbol and installation of labyrinths since 1994. He is a Principal and Co-Founder of the LAByrinth Xperience, a human dynamic that accelerates change and creativity; and creator of FourSquare Rapid Design System. Joe has reframed the ancient concept of the labyrinth  into an emergent model for the 21ˢᵗ century that facilitates practical wisdom for organizations and individuals. He has presented throughout the world and brings his experience as an art educator and TV director into developing programs for clients, including Dupont, Area Energy, DeAgostini Publishing Group, IT, Exxon, Federal Express, EURO RSCG worldwide, University of Tennessee leadership program, New Haven University MBA leadership program, and the Center for Creative Leadership, among others. He is a founding member and a member of the first board of directors of the Labyrinth Society, and a colleague and member of the Creative Problem Solving Institute and the American Creativity Association.

Tricia Pearce, BSW, M.Ed.

Tricia is Principal and Co-Founder of the LAByrinth Xperience, the original work that is the foundation of Mountain 10. She brings her unique experience utilizing labyrinths in personal reflection, spiritual discernment and team-building across the United States and around the world to facilitate programs for business, conferences and retreat centers. She leads with passionate commitment to openness, inclusion, capacity building and action. Her work in hospital administration for over 20 years garnered several awards for innovative programming in Trauma Aftercare, Reiki for Patients and Pet Therapy. She served as President of the New England and Connecticut Associations of Volunteer Services. Tricia currently works as a consultant, facilitator and coach.

Made in the USA
Lexington, KY
28 April 2018